# inner EXCAVATION

## Explore Your Self Through
## Photography, Poetry and Mixed Media

Liz Lamoreux

**NORTH LIGHT BOOKS**
Cincinnati, Ohio

Published by North Light Books, an imprint of F+W Media, Inc., 4700 East Galbraith Road, Cincinnati, Ohio 45236. (800) 289-0963. First edition.

14  13  12 11  10   5 4 3 2 1

Distributed in Canada by Fraser Direct
100 Armstrong Avenue
Georgetown, ON, Canada  L7G 5S4
Tel: (905) 877-4411

Distributed in the U.K. and Europe by F+W Media
International
Brunel House, Newton Abbot, Devon, TQ12 4PU,
England
Tel: (+44) 1626 323200, Fax: (+44) 1626 323319
E-mail: postmaster@davidandcharles.co.uk

Distributed in Australia by Capricorn Link
P.O. Box 704, S. Windsor, NSW 2756 Australia
Tel: (02) 4577-3555

          Library of Congress Cataloging-in-Publication
Data

Lamoreux, Liz.
   Inner excavation / Liz Lamoreux. -- 1st ed.
       p. cm.
   Includes bibliographical references and index.
   ISBN-13: 978-1-4403-0309-8 (pbk. : alk. paper)
   ISBN-10: 1-4403-0309-6 (pbk. : alk. paper)
   1.  Lamoreux, Liz--Meditations. 2.  Artisans--United
States--Psychology.  I. Title.
   TT140.L36A3 2010
   745.092--dc22
                              2010012992

www.fwmedia.com

**Editor:** Tonia Davenport

**Cover Designer:** Michelle Thompson

**Interior Designer:** Geoff Raker

**Layout Designer:** Ronson Slagle

**Production Coordinator:** Greg Nock

# DEDICATION

To Grandma & Grandpa Nord:
For taking my hand, even now, and
showing me how to live.

# GRATITUDE

The beautiful contributors to *Inner Excavation*: Through your examples, art and truth, I have learned so much. Thank you for all that you have given this book.

Tonia: Thank you for the nudge to get my ideas onto paper and then the endless patience as this book came into being.

Jenna: Thank you for your support throughout this experience and for your eagle eyes and kind words.

My circle of women: Your gentle reminders, invitations to look in the mirror, pushes to speak my truth and love light my path. Thank you.

Mom: Thank you for teaching me to stand tall in this life and for being there, always.

Dad: Thank you for showing me that no matter the path behind, you can always find your way.

Millie: My constant companion as I write, create and edit, thank you for your example of love.

Jon: I am so blessed to walk beside you in this life. Thank you for your encouragement and love as I live my dreams into reality.

Eleanore Jane: You have already taught me so much about bravery and love. I am so lucky to be your mamma.

# CONTENTS

# JOURNEY INWARD

I am so glad to find you here reading these words because it means you are in the midst of one of the greatest adventures of your life—looking inward and sifting through the layers to unearth who you are as you walk on your life's path. The journey of doing this work—the big work—of looking inward to figure out where you are, where you want to go, how you got to this moment, is the focus of this book.

We explore this inner journey through three mediums: photography, poetry and mixed-media art. Each chapter examines a theme that focuses on the self—including topics like looking at the past and exploring the body. Through the exercises in this book, you will begin to play in the world of self-portraits. And you will not be alone; contributing artists will share their insights and examples of their own self-discoveries through their artwork and writing in each chapter. You will also be invited to pay attention to the clues that you find on your excavation. My hope is that you will literally keep an "Excavator's Notebook" to write down your insights and ideas as they are shown to you. Then, you can reflect on these notes to notice any themes, hopes and whispered truths. These ideas will often become the artifacts that push you to create, capture your world through photography and write.

A few other details: You will find that the chapters are divided into three areas of focus: photography, poetry and mixed media. Note that the photography and poetry sections throughout the book open with prompts. With each of these prompts, there might be an obvious connection to the theme of the chapter, the prompt might provide another tool to add to your creative toolbox,

or the exercise might simply push you to get out of your head and take some action. The goal of all the prompts and exercises in this book is for you to have fun as you use your creative journey to reveal more about who you are.

Each mixed-media section features art that's inspired by the chapter topic. While specific how-to instruction for creating the work is not included, it is my hope that you will be motivated to create with the materials that you personally are passionate about and that you will begin to think about how photography and poetry can shape what and how you create.

I also want to introduce to you the importance of balancing the creative inner work with time spent in the quiet as you come across "Delving into the Quiet" exercises and other meditations. I believe that introducing self-care through this quiet, even if just for a minute or two, can help us seek a balance in our lives. Note that I say *seek* and not *find*. I am not sure we truly ever find a balance like the young boy who ventures atop the seasaw in a childhood physics experiment as he walks toward the middle until the seasaw balances, his arms lifted in triumph. Rather, I believe that when we seek this balance with the intention of giving ourselves, our minds, our hectic lives, and for some, our over-thinking tendencies a breather, we can be more fully present. Present as we look inward but also as we go about our daily lives.

Although this deep inner work—the heavy lifting as I often call it—can be difficult at times and push us in unexpected ways, I believe you will find yourself standing amidst joy and possibility as you uncover pieces of you.

Let's begin . . . .

# CHAPTER 1: *I begin*

This chapter is your invitation to begin the journey of looking inward to find where you are on your path and where you want to go. You will explore words and the world around you, and you will add tools to your creative toolbox as you begin to give more attention to the moments that make up your life. These tools will help you begin to document this path, these moments, this life that you live.

A few years ago, the word *begin* appeared everywhere I turned. I was in the midst of a cracking open that would unlock a part of me I hadn't listened to in many years. It was a time when life simply took over and said, "Even though this isn't going to be fun, it is where you are going. So hold on. But keep your eyes open or you might miss the good parts."

My husband and I had moved across the country from our friends and family; I was working from home and struggling to meet people in our new community; and several loved ones in our lives were diagnosed with cancer or were ill. Then, over a five-month period, three of these loved ones died. I found myself on the journey of deep, wide grief for the first time in my life. It was not the path I wanted to be on. I felt alone and lost and unsure.

As I kept holding on, or rather, trying to hold my heart together, I found myself drawn to a few creative blogs I had stumbled across online. These women were trying to make sense of their worlds. They were sharing their stories and invited a sense of community through this sharing. Many of these women were also focusing on ways to bring creating and art into their lives; some were even full-time artists. As I read their brave, open words, I started to hear a whisper that sounded a bit like, "You are not alone."

Have you had that experience? Finding yourself lost in a book or a conversation with a friend and hearing that whispered truth that you are not alone? As I read those blogs and then gathered a few treasured books that had sat on my bookshelves unopened for several years, I began to wonder if I could be a part of this community.

This wondering caused me to pay attention to where I wanted to go. I began to listen and push myself to realize that my days could be shaped by playing and learning and looking in the midst of working and doing the "things I needed to do." It was during these moments that the word *begin* started to appear.

Could I really start a blog? Could I really admit I wanted to write? Could I gather paints and paper and play?

The answer that repeatedly came through the words I read and the conversations I had was "Just begin. Begin. Begin. Now."

I started my blog. I began to carry my camera with me and go on "Artist Dates" (as talked about in Julia Cameron's book *The Artist's Way*). Through my blog, I began to document the pieces of my journey as I looked at where I stood in my life, the path behind me and where I wanted to go.

As I did this, I found myself noticing a joy within. It was as though my innermost self was nodding and saying, "Yes. This is it." I began to realize that the new adventure of listening to myself, paying attention and deciding to really live in my life had become the gift within my grief.

In this chapter, you will examine ways to capture the simple moments of your life with your camera and look at what insight you can glean from these photographs. You will peek into the world of poetry as you discover the idea of a "Word Toolbox" and begin to write. You will also look at how photographs and poetry can push you to create artwork from within. As you read this chapter, I hope you will pause to listen to the thoughts that emerge. I hope you will notice your inner invitations telling you to begin. Think about writing down these thoughts as they whisper and maybe even roar.

## Tools for the Journey:
### Inspired Reading

The books I gathered included:

*Long Quiet Highway* by Natalie Goldberg

*Succulent Wild Woman* by SARK

*Mostly True* by Brian Andreas

*The Awakening* by Kate Chopin

*Night Noises* by Crockett Johnston

*The Cloister Walk* by Kathleen Norris

*The Artist's Way* by Julia Cameron

*Spilling Open* by Sabrina Ward Harrison

# Seeking Light and Shadow

A few months into writing my blog, I found myself taking photos of moments throughout my day. I began to carry my camera with me almost all the time so that I could capture the light and colors of my world. As the years have passed, my camera has begun to feel like an extension of me as I seek the details through my lens, such as the swirling tea inside a teacup while enjoying a moment with a friend, or discover the feeling of a moment mirrored back at me, such as when I notice an unexpected reflection. In this section, you look at the patterns and clues that can be found in capturing these moments with your camera.

# PHOTO EXCURSION:
# SCENES FROM THIS DAY

We begin this section with an exercise that encourages you to record moments from one day in your life. In doing this, you will find yourself seeing your everyday world with new eyes.

**TASK:** Document one day in your life in photographs. Take your camera with you throughout the day and snap photos of moments within this day.

**NOTES:** The truth is that taking photos on a birthday party day or a day spent at the zoo is something you probably already do. The challenge instead is to choose an ordinary day and then to invite yourself to really look at what you see in your world.

PHOTOS BY LIZ LAMOREUX

**EXAMPLES:** The photos you see here and on the following two pages represent one autumn Sunday in my world. Note that I didn't worry too much about taking the perfect photo. I like how some of these are somewhat blurry because quiet Sundays feel a bit like this. The photo of Millie, our golden retriever, wasn't "the best one" of the set I took when she put her head in my lap. Yet, it captured our little family cozy together by the fireplace; Jon works in the background on his computer and you can see a bit of a favorite quilt on my lap. I often put a set like this on my blog to capture the scenes from a day so that when I look back, I will remember the little daily nuances.

As I carry my camera with me, I find that giving myself specific assignments helps me to document and sift through my experiences and pushes me to be a bit more creative with what I choose to photograph. Sometimes I will try to find certain colors on a given day or work on a series of self-portraits. Other days, I begin to notice a pattern within my photographs that births a series of photos I begin to take. For example, while looking through the photos I had taken on a trip back to the Midwest, I noticed several shadow and reflection photos of my husband and me. This has led to a new series of photos that I enjoy taking when we explore the world together (see a few of these shadow photos on pages 89–91).

**PHOTOS BY LIZ LAMOREUX**

The idea of a photo series can be interpreted in many ways. In this chapter, you look at a few different examples. In the previous "Photography Excursion" exercise, you looked at the idea of "Scenes from This Day" to document one day in your life. The end product is indeed a photography series.

The following series of photos from Jen Goff represent two different "moments of quiet" in the midst of a week. Both series give an intimate look into these moments in Jen's life. One is almost drawn to take a deep breath when looking at these photos as each one evokes an invitation to pause.

The first series shows a glimpse into the first moments in a morning.

The second series was taken in the afternoon while Jen had a break in the midst of a meditation retreat.

Both of Jen's photo series have a slight peek of a self-portrait through the hands and feet, which adds another layer of intimacy to these sets. Note the lighting, reflections and shadows.

Consider how you might express who you are through a series of photos.

**PHOTOS BY JEN GOFF**

# ARTIST ILLUMINATION
## INTERVIEW WITH JEN GOFF

Here is a glimpse into how Jen sees herself.

**Who are you?**
*I am*
*silhouette*
*old barn*
*mist and fog*
*beauty unfolding*
*slowly untangling*
*whispers*
*songs*
*new guitar strings*

**Who or what inspires you?**
Artists:
Mary Ellen Mark (photographer)
Chelsea Heffner (artist)

Books/Authors:
*Writing Down the Bones* by Natalie Goldberg
*Spilling Open* by Sabrina Ward Harrison
Mary Oliver (poet/writer)

Music:
Sigur Rós
Rachel's

JEN'S RESPONSE TO "WHO ARE YOU?"

**How do you nurture yourself?**
I nurture myself with pen and paper in a café, with the movement of my hands, creating something new. I nurture myself by long baths, walks through the art museum and morning meditations.

**How did you find your creative voice?**
It took me a long time to hear any creative voice. It came in slow whispers; I kept trying. I cannot name a day that it came to me, it just came in moments, with the help of other artists urging me along and a feeling that every fiber of my being needed to create.

# BEHIND THE LENS:
# IN A SERIES

Explore what it means to take photos in a series while seeking a common thread amidst these photos.

**TASK:** Spend time brainstorming a theme, location, time period and so on for a photo series. Then, capture that series with your camera.

**NOTES:** Some ideas to get you started:

- Take photos of your morning cup of tea or coffee.
- Photograph cupcakes in all the cities you visit.
- Document the scene outside a favorite window at home at the same time for a set period of time: weekly, once a month and so on. Notice how the light changes.
- Find a tree on your walk home from school with your children, and snap a photo every now and then.
- Take photos of your hands holding different objects: rocks, flowers, a mug, someone's hand.
- Take one photo a day for a specified time period.

Contributor Kristen Perman often walks in New York City with her camera at the ready. These walks have created an entire series of city photos in her portfolio that represents seasons, energies and textures of this much beloved city she calls "part of her heart." The following photos are from one of her winter walks.

At the train station near her home, Kristen's solitary photo walk ritual begins. With the first photo snapped, she feels invited to shed the labels of wife, mom, acupuncturist and so on and identify again as just Kristen. While she walks the streets of New York, she is drawn to the architecture and the history. She feels as though she is finding the stories in the faded paint on the bricks and signs and water towers. Even though part of what draws her to New York is its vibrancy at all moments of the day, she seeks to capture its history through her lens.

**PHOTOS BY KRISTEN PERMAN**

## BEHIND THE LENS:
# TAKE A WALK

Taking a walk with your camera can become a way to practice mindfulness and simply enjoy the present moment.

**TASK:** Let your camera be your companion as you take a walk in a familiar or an unfamiliar corner of the world.

**NOTES:** You might simply want to walk around your neighborhood, and look with new eyes at the trees, sidewalk cracks and buildings you pass each day. If you live in a city, consider finding a nature preserve or place out in the country where you can walk. If you live in a more suburban or rural area, travel to the nearest big city, and visit the downtown area to see what you can see. Let these focused-in moments, found by your lens, push you to see your world with new eyes.

17

# Revealing the Poet Within

In this section, you will dip your toes into the world of poetry and play with words. You will discover the joys of having a Word Toolbox and learn about how having words available in front of you makes it so much easier to free the poet within you. Even if poetry hasn't always had a place on a shelf in your home, I encourage you to read on (because I just know you will discover the poems that live inside you).

## WORDS DISCOVERED:
# CREATING A WORD TOOLBOX

A favorite book that makes poetry accessible is *poemcrazy* by Susan Wooldridge. I was lucky enough to take a class from Susan in 2007. After her workshop, I began to realize that a writer can have a "toolbox of words" available to make the writing experience just a little bit easier. This toolbox doesn't refer to the words we carry around in our heads at any given moment. Instead, this toolbox can come in the form of lists of words, pages literally torn out of old dictionaries, journals filled with phrases. This toolbox becomes a mine holding just the right word that can lead to just the right phrase to begin a poem.

**TASK:** Gather words and begin to create a Word Toolbox.

**NOTES:** Grab a book off your bookshelf (the first one you see is a good place to start). Open to random pages and write down a word or two from each page. It is a good idea to let your eyes jump from word to word to find the word that stands out to you. Write down at least twenty words. Look at your word list. Is it interesting to you? Do the words jump out? Do they make you think? Do you feel a desire to pick up your pencil and write? If not, I invite you to try this exercise again, perhaps with another book. This time, look for words that are juicy, beautiful, messy, sticky, solid. Look for words that invite images of action and stillness. Look for words that twirl around on your tongue. Write down the word that scares you, makes you smile and invites you to say, "Yes!" Do not be afraid of the word you do not know; add it to your list. Begin to collect your words in an accessible location. Maybe tape them in your journal, gather them in a document on your computer, or create a special Word Toolbox from an old cigar box or basket. The key is to be able to find them quickly when you want to write. Think about other places where you might find words:

- Go to a thrift store and buy an old dictionary. When you sit down to write, rip out a page (really, you can do it) to use as your word list.
- Use vocabulary cards (you can buy these at a bookstore or online) and gather a few in a pile as part of your Word Toolbox.
- Visit the library and make word lists from the books you find there.
- When you are finished with a magazine, rip out a few articles, grab a favorite pen and circle the words that stand out to you in the articles.

As you write down your words, I invite you to pause before capturing an entire phrase verbatim because that phrase really belongs to the author of whatever you are reading.

The first time I remember really thinking about poetry was when I read Carl Sandburg's poem "Fog" in the fourth grade. I recall attempting to visualize fog arriving like cat's feet, but as a northern Indiana girl, I struggled with this image. To me, fog was thick and never-ending and meant being really quiet in the backseat as one of my parents drove at night. Now, living in the Pacific Northwest, I can close my eyes and see fog stepping quickly, lightly, yet solidly across Puget Sound, and I smile with an understanding of Sandburg's choice of words.

Poetry continued to come in and out of my life in positive ways (an eighth-grade girl's attempt to make sense of the world through poetry, a teenager memorizing Langston Hughes' "Theme for English B") until my senior year in high school when it suddenly seemed inaccessible and, well, hard to understand. Poetry, or at least "academic poetry," and I took a break.

Then, in my late twenties I read Derek Walcott's poem "Love After Love" and everything shifted. This poem held up a mirror and seemed to say, "Look closer." I soon found myself in the poetry section of a local bookstore sitting on the floor with Mary Oliver and Sharon Olds and Billy Collins, and again, I heard the whispers, "You are not alone."

Through the encouragement of an online community of others who appreciated, wrote and read poetry, I began writing poems as part of my writing practice. I also started sharing some of them on my blog.

Now this is the part where I am concerned I might lose you. What I have learned is that many people have had experiences like I did in high school where poetry simply becomes inaccessible. We read a poem and feel like we just "don't get it." Then a teacher tells us what the poem is supposed to mean, and we sit there thinking, "Seriously? I do not get poetry."

If this sounds like your experience, please know you are in the right place. In this chapter, we simply begin with *words*.

When I explained to Susan Tuttle that I wanted her to gather words to create a poem for this chapter, she surprised me with the explanation that she already does this. Before she writes, she gathers words from her vintage book collection to use as prompts and inspiration for her writing. "Lodging of the Heart" is Susan's poem inspired by collected words.

## LODGING OF THE HEART
Susan Tuttle

*cloaked in blessed guard*
*is the lodging of the heart;*
*a home of deep and steady joy;*
*where pain is mere scrawls etched on the walls of*
*spirit—self-deceiving fear that bows to*
*imagined superiors.*

*As she turns her face inward*
*toward stillness*
*she glimpses worth and wishes self-denied,*
*shimmering below the current,*
*like gold coins carved with enchanted things like*
*butterflies, garlands and stars;*
*she recognizes them as her birthright*
*all hers*
*waiting to be grasped and*
*embraced.*

Finding words in unexpected places is a great way to not only bring in words you might not use on a regular basis but also to push yourself to find another way to say a phrase or evoke a feeling. Imagine finding words in a chemistry textbook or your child's favorite book or a cooking magazine. Using a vintage book might reintroduce you to words you haven't heard used since your childhood or teach you words from the childhoods of your grandparents.

## ON THE PAGE:
# JUST WRITE

Your Word Toolbox becomes a source of inspiration and word possibilities for your writing as you seek the poetry within you.

**TASK:** Gather your Word Toolbox and use one of the following prompts as a starting point for writing some "poetic phrases" that are probably going to look and read a lot like a poem:

- I begin . . .
- I am . . .
- I stand . . .
- I see a woman/a man . . .

**NOTES:** Use words from your Word Toolbox to get started or when you get stuck. String those words together and see where they take you. If it feels more comfortable to change "I" to "she" or "he," please do so. You will note Susan's poem is in the third person and retains an intimacy that these prompts invite. Think about similar two- or three-word phrases that begin with I (or she/he) that could be additional prompts for your writing. Hint: Each chapter title in this book could be a prompt for this exercise.

# Unearthing Your
# Artistic Adventurer

In this section, you will look at how you can use your words and photos to inspire a mixed-media creation. If you felt at all intimidated by the poetry and photography exercises so far, I invite you to read about contributor Kelly Barton's experience walking through these prompts in mediums she is not as comfortable with before heading into her studio to create in the environment where she feels more at ease. Maybe you will be inspired to create a collage or another mixed-media piece that represents where you are as you begin this journey toward the inner you.

When I talked to Kelly Barton about creating a mixed-media piece for this chapter, I asked if she might be open to following poetry and photography prompts as a starting point before creating her painting. Her response was something along the lines of, "You want me to write a poem? I do not write poetry." I loved this response. She patiently listened as I explained what I meant. A word list. Stringing those words together as the beginnings of a poem. "I could totally do that," she said.

Kelly started with the poetry prompt of taking a book down from her bookshelf and writing a word list. She then used the words to create this poem:

*i am me . . .*
*me, patchouli, sunny, tiny bewigged, me*
*warhol factory silly betty creative, me*
*to be uninhibited, authentic, fearless*
*me. glamorous outsider, resilient, free.*

In the past few months, Kelly has begun to play with self-portrait photography. She has made it a goal to learn more about how to use her camera and which lens works best for the moments she wants to capture. When I asked her to take a series of photos, she was drawn to take several mirror self-portraits that represent different emotions and moods she experienced throughout one day.

**PHOTOS BY KELLY BARTON**

23

ARTWORK BY KELLY BARTON

Although the poem and the photos are not directly part of the mixed-media painting, the experience of taking the photos and writing the poem influenced the mood Kelly created in this piece. She pulled the word "free" from her poem and used it in painting to illustrate the idea of simply being herself and being true to the person she is. She pushed herself to let go of her preconceived notions of self-portraits as well as of herself. Through her artwork, she expresses what she learned from this experience, which is part of the freedom she feels when she creates.

# ARTIST ILLUMINATION
## INTERVIEW WITH KELLY BARTON

Here is a glimpse into how Kelly sees herself.

**Who are you?**
*i am*
> *a frida-loving*
> > *sassy irish maiden*

*a silly inappropriate creative*

> *a brave warrior girl*

*sunny betty laughter*

> *i am a gypsy*
> > *life explorer*

*i am*
> *beloved. free. girl.*

KELLY'S RESPONSE TO "WHO ARE YOU?"

**Who or what inspires you?**
Books/Authors:
*The Prophet* by Kahlil Gibran
I was just introduced to the poet David Whyte.
When his poem "Sweet Darkness" was read to
me, I simply felt: Home.

Music:
"Redemption Song" by Bob Marley

**How do you nurture yourself?**
Kelly + Nurture = Nap!

**How did you find your creative voice?**
I feel like she (my creative voice) has
always been there, but after years of
ignoring her, the gypsy decided it was
long overdue and she needed to come
out and play. Pretty happy she did!

# IN THE STUDIO:
# A COLLAGE OF YOU

This is your permission slip to begin creating a piece of art inspired by your words and photos.

**TASK:** Create a mixed-media collage using the photos you have taken and the poetry you have written in this chapter.

**NOTES:** You might want to simply use the photos and poetry as inspiration or you might want to add them directly into your collage.

Other things to consider:

- Is there an art medium you've wanted to play with but haven't?
- How might you incorporate your words and photos into a medium you already feel comfortable with?
- If the idea of "choosing" an art medium seems overwhelming, try this: Give yourself the gift of a new box of crayons, a blank unlined journal, some glue and a few new fun pens. Print out your series photos. Begin to simply have fun with these tools as you create with your own words, images and color.

## Tools for the Journey:
### Kelly's Collage Tips

A few ideas to get you started with collage:

SUBSTRATE: Decide what you will use as the base for your collage. You might begin with a standard canvas or a piece of watercolor paper. However, you could also think outside the box and use an old wooden tray, a vintage frame, corrugated cardboard, scraps of wood or old book covers. (Note that gesso is a great way to prime your surface if needed.)

COLLAGE PAPERS: Here are some of my favorite non-traditional paper sources: magazine pages, children's catalogs, food and beverage labels or pieces of mail.

GLUE: I usually use gel medium. There are several out there (from glossy to matte); experiment to find the one that you like best. When you are creating just for fun, consider using a glue stick or regular Elmer's Glue.

PAINT AND OTHER MEDIUMS: What I love most about mixed media is the freedom to use different mediums within the same painting. I often use graphite for outlining and layering under the paint. A few paint options to think about:

- If you are just starting out, try craft acrylics. They are inexpensive and great to practice with (many experienced artists use them all the time).
- Liquitex and Golden are more expensive but have different textures and weights than the less expensive paints. The pigments and coverage can be richer as well.
- Many acrylic brands also carry complementary mediums such as molding paste, granulars and finishes. These can assist in layers and texturing.

READY TO START? Here are some thoughts:

- Collage your background with various papers, graphics and stamped images.
- Give the background a wash of color.
- Gel medium can be used to transfer photos (there are several tutorials on the Internet).
- Fabrics, ribbon and lace are perfect additions to backgrounds or finishing touches.

DON'T FORGET: Allow yourself to create freely. Don't focus on how you "think" you have to do it. Experiment and enjoy the process.

# Delving Into the Quiet:

# A PERSONAL PRACTICE

Each day, I try to bring moments of quiet and ritual into my life. Many mornings, I begin the day with a cup of tea and a lit candle, then I write a few pages in my journal and then stretch and breathe my way into the day with a few yoga poses. When dusk arrives early in the fall and winter, I light candles throughout the house to bring in the light. While I light these candles, I think of people in my life and send out blessings to them. These moments are part of my personal practice and act as bookends to the ebb and flow of my days.

The quiet of these moments also invites a balance in my life. When I am writing just to let the thoughts escape my very chatty brain or stretching my body to awaken it, I am not running ahead to the next project, blog post, idea. When you are in the habit of pushing yourself to unearth the reasons and feelings behind where you are on your path, you also need to give yourself the gift of the quiet, the rest, the repetition of comfort and self-care.

I invite you to think about the things you already do that make up your personal practice. Maybe you write morning pages as prescribed by Julia Cameron in *The Artist's Way*. Maybe you go for a daily walk or take a break in the middle of the day with a book and cup of tea. Perhaps you run or practice yoga. Think about what you already do that is part of your practice. Think about what you might like to add to a daily practice.

# CHAPTER 2: *I seek*

Now that we are ready to begin this journey of *Inner Excavation*, let's take a trip to the days before today to think about what brought us to this moment and our decision to look inward for answers. As we seek clues from the past in this chapter, we take three important things with us: a flashlight, the senses and who we are in this moment.

During my junior year in high school, we spent the entire year looking at three questions: Where do we come from? Where are we? Where are we going? Since then, I have often turned to these questions in my own life. In my early twenties, I admit to focusing more on "where I want to go," but my experience has been that with age comes a desire to investigate what led me to this moment—this place on my path. Now, my writing and art are steeped in this inner work of looking back as I try to make sense of where I am and where I want to go. With some of my work, I try to honor the whispers of those who came before me as I play with pieces of the past and discover tools my grandmothers and great-grandmothers used in their daily domestic creating.

Do you notice the whispers of those who came before you? Are you drawn to investigate your past? For some of us, looking at the past brings up "stuff." Sometimes this "stuff" is filled with images, memories and experiences that we don't want to investigate. Although I believe there is power in shining light on the experiences that came before this moment, know that for the purposes of this book, you are in charge of your journey into the past.

As you are invited to look back in this chapter, do so in the way that feels right to you as you use a flashlight to look at the path behind you to see what it holds. This image of a flashlight is to remind you that you are shining light onto your past and that you are in control of where you venture with this light. Perhaps you will want to look back to last week or last year. Perhaps you will want to revisit the days of your childhood or your child's younger years. However far back you want to go is up to you. Just remember, you can always come back to this moment to feel the light of today that shines on your path.

## The Excavator's Notebook:
### Your Past

Hearing the words "your past" sometimes brings about a strong reaction. Perhaps you are comfortable looking behind you to investigate. Maybe you see examining the past as looking backwards when you want to stand firmly in the present and look toward the future. Spend some time writing about the thoughts that emerge for you. Consider what enters your mind when you think about "investigating your past."

In this chapter, exploration of the senses is another tool you will add to your creative toolbox. The beauty of using the senses as a tool for creativity is that you always have them with you. You can use them to soak up a moment so you can remember small details. You can draw on them to capture a photograph or paint a picture when you write. To me, the senses are a tool to help us live more richly in our lives. However, when you start to notice your senses in a conscious way, it might seem that you use only one or two in any given moment. You might notice you are more sensitive to one sense over the others. As you explore the senses, become an observer of yourself and how you use your senses in your creative adventures.

You might be wondering what the senses have to do with examining the past as part of the inward journey. In this chapter, as you peek into the past, you will use the senses as a guide to tap into memories in a gentle way. You will also use them to imagine what moments from the past might have been like for those who came before you. You will investigate the senses of now through photography and then spend time sifting through photos of the past. You will write about the senses of your memories and how this can reveal new clues to you about where you are. You will also discover ways to incorporate the past, and what you are drawn to about the past, into your artwork.

# *Delving Into the Quiet:*

# A SENSES MEDITATION

Find a quiet place to comfortably sit. Let both of your feet rest gently on the floor so you can literally feel the earth beneath you. Take a moment to come into your body.

Close your eyes. Your shoulders drop away from your ears, the muscles of your face relax. Find your breath.

With each inhalation, feel your chest expand. With each exhalation, drop deeper into your body. Spend a few breath cycles noticing this.

When you are ready, begin to notice:

What you see

What you hear

What you smell

What you taste

What you feel

Breathe in all of this until the experience of this moment rests inside you.

When you are ready, open your eyes and notice the effects of this experience:

On your body

On your mind

On your heart

**NOTES:** Before beginning any of the meditations introduced in this book, I invite you to give yourself permission to find a room where you are alone and know you will not be interrupted. You can also create a walking meditation from this exercise. Instead of sitting and closing your eyes, find a place to walk where you will not be interrupted. Find a comfortable, somewhat slow walking pace and begin to find your breath. Then, follow along with the rest of the meditation.

# Seeking Light and Shadow

As we get ready to embark on this trip to the past, I want to remind you again that you control the areas of the past you wish to explore. As you examine photos from last week or fifty years ago, you do so with the gift of today's perspective. My belief is that this perspective illuminates the path behind us so we can begin to find ourselves in this moment in our lives. Before we begin to look behind us though, we spend time using the senses to explore a way to be present in our lives now.

# PHOTOGRAPHY EXCURSION:
# SENSES WARM UP

For the last few years, I have used the five physical senses plus a sixth sense of "know" as a jumping-off point for a few creative exercises. Some of these exercises have become part of a "Senses" series on my blog. They began as writing exercises to capture a moment. Somewhere along the way, I also began taking photos that represented the senses of a moment. This photography exercise recharges my creative well and pushes me to leave my home office and studio (even if this just means to the backyard) to capture the world around me through the lens.

**TASK:** Capture the senses around you through photos. Consider the following ideas:

• Go for a nature walk and find the senses.

• Head to your favorite coffee shop and soak up the senses through your lens.

• Spend time with a friend and capture the senses of your time together.

• Explore the senses of one object, such as a tree or rosebush, a cup of tea, a favorite spot in your home. This is what I did for the example photographs you see here and those on the next page.

**NOTES:** As mentioned previously in my own senses explorations, I include a sixth sense of "know" that illustrates something I "know" in this moment. You might want to also add this sixth sense to your series. As you take your photos, you might find that you are literally seeking what you can hear, taste, smell. This is fine. I also encourage you to go for a more abstract interpretation of the senses. Perhaps take several photos of an experience and then later find the senses within the photos. In my "Hear" example, I was not literally hearing the flowers when I took the photo, but when I examined the photos later, the way the flowers looked upward toward the blue sky made

me think about how you can almost hear them stretching as they reach toward the sun.

**EXAMPLE:** The following photos are my own senses exploration while taking photos of one dahlia plant at the Dahlia Garden at Point Defiance Park in my town.

**Touch**

**Hear**

PHOTOS BY LIZ LAMOREUX

**See**

**Smell**

**Taste**

PHOTOS BY LIZ LAMOREUX

**Know**

When I attended ArtFest (an incredible art retreat in the Pacific Northwest) for the first time a few years ago, two of the materials lists for workshops I took listed "photocopies of vintage photos, a few old letters and old postcards." I didn't think I had many letters and photos, but I managed to make photocopies of a few family letters I had squirreled away and photos of my great-grandparents, grandparents and me as a little girl. I was so proud of the little stash of "vintage ephemera" that I had gathered.

A few minutes into this first workshop, I quickly discovered that the instructor did not mean the photos and letters needed to be from my own past. I looked around and listened as students showed one another the supplies they had, and I realized that those savvy, experienced mixed-media artists were experts at finding vintage photos and letters at thrift stores and flea markets. Even though at the time I felt a bit silly, creating with these pieces of my own past was the beginning of an important understanding of what I am drawn to on my own creative journey: I am drawn to items that whisper stories from my past. I am drawn to the stories of the women who came before me. I am drawn to writing these stories—to writing my own story. When I realized this, I began an excavation into my own past.

The exploration of my own past began with photographs because they are tangible and visual pieces of where I come from. When my grandfather died in 2009 and we gathered at his home for the last time, several of the family photos and letters were scanned so that even if they were divided among family members, we would have digital copies. Because of these scans, I now treasure a copy of a photo-booth strip my grandparents took while on their honeymoon and an incredible photo of my great-grandmother (who inspires my sewing excursions) in overalls in the 1930s.

After exploring the photos on my mom's side of the family, I asked my dad if my grandmother had any family photos she might share with me, and during my next visit home, I suddenly found myself staring at the young, mischievous face of the grandfather I had never known. My father's father died before I was born, and I had seen only a few photos of him. I listened as my dad reflected on his past and explained that as a child, he thought his father looked like James Dean. I saw the Christmas card photo of my dad and his brothers from the late 1940s. My grandmother shared story after story about family gatherings and the time she stood looking at Lake Michigan frozen in the 1950s. During these moments, I realized how many pieces of my own past I would have never known if I hadn't simply asked the question, "Dad, does Grandma have some photos I can scan?"

When I don't have specific memories of an experience, I look for clues in photos, such as in this photo of my great-grandfather and me. Looking closely, I see that my mother and I brought him Fannie Mae candies, which is the box we are opening; I recognize the wrapping. Another clue in this photo: Even though he hadn't been behind a tractor in years, the farmer is present as evidenced by his hat that says, "DeKalb," a Midwest feed company.

When I first saw this photo of my mother, I thought it was me. After hearing, "You look so much like your father" for my entire life, I suddenly had the gift of also seeing myself in my mother's face.

33

# The Excavator's Notebook:
## An Awakening

Have you had an experience that awakened a desire to uncover what inspires your creativity? Perhaps you have found yourself in a workshop or playing in your studio or writing in your journal or on a photography adventure and suddenly realized you are having more fun than you thought possible. Write about that experience and what it taught you. Think about what you are drawn to create with/write about/photograph and why.

My mother's parents on their honeymoon as the world waits for them to leave their mark.

When I looked at this photo of my father and his two brothers for the first time, I was struck by the way you can see their children in their faces.

Oh how I love the overalls in this photo of my great-grandmother and my great-aunt and how the car places the scene in the early 1930s.

## BEHIND THE LENS:
# SIFTING THROUGH IMAGES OF THE PAST

Peek into your personal history as you discover and reexamine family photographs and reflect on what these photos reveal about where you come from.

**TASK:** Spend time sifting through photos from your past. Consider looking at photos of last month, last year, a decade ago, your childhood, photos of those who came before you. Look for patterns and clues that might give you unexpected insight.

**NOTES:** You might not have many photos to look through. Perhaps your parents still have them or maybe you aren't sure where family photos are kept. Perhaps you haven't taken many photos throughout your life. Consider embarking on an investigation to find them. Ask your older relatives; ask your siblings. You might be surprised to find they kept all the photos your parents sent with Christmas cards or that someone has the one photo of the farmhouse you heard stories about but never visited or that your brother has been taking photographs for years but thought you didn't want to see them. Remember that you carry your flashlight with you to shine light on what you choose to see.

## BEHIND THE LENS:
# LANDSCAPE OF HOME

When you visit places that remind you of home and bring your camera, you can look for clues and hidden insights as you explore your surroundings.

**TASK:** Take a trip to places from your past and capture them through your lens. For example:
• Visit a favorite park or another spot in nature that you remember.
• When you visit your parents or grandparents, take photos of some of the details of their home and yard.
• If you live in your hometown, visit your old school grounds and other locations that were daily places in your childhood. Or plan a visit to your hometown to capture some favorite spots.

**NOTES:** This exercise is called "Landscape of Home" because it references contributing artist Darlene Kreutzer's explanation of why she is drawn to take photos of the places of her past (read more about this in the "Revealing the Poet Within" section of this chapter). Think about what landscapes appear in your own memories. Perhaps those images will be a place to start when you gather your camera for this adventure.

If you are unable to visit the landscapes of your past, consider seeking places in your current hometown that remind you of the past.

# Revealing the Poet Within

You will now continue to explore where you come from while carrying your flashlight; this time, you do so in the world of poetry. As you look at the past, you will examine not only where you have traveled, but also the worlds of those who came before you. Through the written word, you will use the senses once again to seek clues into the moments of today and the whispered memories of the past.

# WORDS DISCOVERED:
# WORD WARM-UP

In the previous section, we explored the senses behind the lens; now, let's look at how we can capture the senses with our words.

**TASK:** In this exercise, you will capture the senses of this moment. Begin with a blank page and then write down all that you hear, taste, smell, see, touch. Write down every detail of each sense. Don't censor yourself, just write.

**NOTES:** Push yourself to let your mind chatter rest and focus solely on each sense one right after the next. You might want to write lists for each sense, or you might find yourself painting an image with your words. The point of this exercise is to get the senses of this moment down on the page. You might want to use this exercise in other places also. For example, visit your favorite café or restaurant, sit outside in your backyard or a park near your home, take out your notebook the next time you are in an airport and so on. Consider also adding a sixth sense of "know" to express what you know in this moment.

**EXAMPLE:** The following is a glimpse into a senses exercise I did while at my favorite coffee shop, where I spent many an hour writing this book:

**Hear:** *Foot taps as the guitars and horn swing. The music digs its way into my heart, which seems to extend into my foot as it tap tap taps. I swing my hips slightly. One side, then the other. My head, oh wait, now the shoulders join in. What if I stood up right now. Right now. And started to dance. Arms raised toward the sky with hips that keep time, boom ba boom ba. The six men playing the music, three feet from our table, would probably love it. Oh how my body wants to do this. Head bops. Foot taps. Breath. Center. A dancer disguised as a writer listening to the Sunday afternoon music at the Mandolin Café.*

**See:** *The soft, yellow light of this café enclosed in Pacific Northwest rain finds people huddled together. Coffee, tea, laughter. They listen. They talk. They write. They read. They trade sections of the Sunday paper. They soak up soup, sandwiches, lasagna. These eyes see contentment on the faces I do not know. Beautiful.*

**Touch:** *Wrapped around the small white mug, my hands feel the warmth of jasmine green seeping through the ceramic. It slides down my throat, and the chill of the day melts away as I settle into this chair and this moment and this life.*

**Smell:** *Breathe deep. Wait. What is there? Hints of coffee, strawberries, jasmine green tea, something bakes in a corner somewhere. I need to spend more time swirling inside what my inhalation finds. Pay attention. This is important. Breathe deep. Wait. Notice.*

**Taste:** *Lettuce swimming with a bouquet of blueberries and strawberries. The specifically pungent blue cheese dances with vinaigrette. Then there is the earthy, dandelion-esque lettuce that makes me want to run into the backyard of my childhood and pull something from the ground just to taste it. My memory cannot find an instance to pull from. My childhood world wasn't an eat something directly from the earth sort of place. A puzzle of sorts as my father ate tomatoes right off the vine standing next to his father, and my mother visited her grandparents' farm, the sort of farm where you planted seeds that grew and found their way to your table. So in this memory, I pretend, eight years old, fictitious grandparents' garden, heads of lettuce begging to be tasted. Eyes turn up to a wrinkled-by-wisdom face that smiles, "Go ahead, Elizabeth."*

**And know:** *A dancer disguised as a writer. A writer disguised as a foot-tapping smile. A longing disguised as a quiet glance. A lover disguised as a sip of tea. In this moment, this is me.*

With the senses as our guide, let's reflect on moments and experiences from the past. Again, "past" can mean last year, a decade ago, when you were five; where you want to visit on your personal timeline is up to you. My belief is that through the senses, we can tiptoe into these memories and suddenly find ourselves unearthing aspects of a moment we never thought we would remember. For example, when freewriting about breakfast at my grandparents' home when I would visit as a child, I suddenly remembered the jelly jar filled with violets and clovers that my grandmother would move from the windowsill to my place setting when I sat down at their kitchen table in the morning. I now fill my own jelly jars with little flowers from the yard and remember her.

Perhaps you want to spend time remembering your child's first Christmas, your mother's cooking, your childhood bedroom. To find the detail, turn this reflection into seeking the sights and textures of your child's first Christmas, the smells and sounds of your mother's kitchen, the texture of the quilt on your childhood bed and the smell of the first perfume on your dresser. With the senses, we dive deeper into the experience and the details begin to fill in the blanks. The phrase, "Remember when we drove all the way to visit Great-Aunt Pearl in Oklahoma" turns into a symphony filled with your brother's laughter in the backseat when you finally got to the punch line of the knock-knock joke, your mother's face filled with joy as she sang along with Conway Twitty on the radio, the specific smells of root beer floats and chili dogs purchased at a drive-in halfway into the trip, the quiet landscape that swirled past your window, the feel of the soft plush blanket when your father covered you up when you began to fall asleep at dusk on day two.

I asked Darlene Kreutzer to reflect on a childhood memory through the senses and to also think about a photograph she might have that illustrated an aspect of this memory. She shared the following poem paired with a photograph.

*barefoot laughter of generations*
*sun on my skin*
*laughter on my side*
*the world blurred and i remembered*
*you,*

*a water sign*
*the smell of life*
*you smiled soft moccasins*
*dancing across the sandy bog*
*your fingers gripping tight*
*tomorrow's feast of spring's stored bounty*

*berries stored*
*medicine for wounds*
*food for bellies*
*water to drink*
*fish to smoke*

*waves lap over rock's wet slip*

*long brown legs*
*dangling off the edge*
*of a blue tailgate*

*a swig of beer*
*a gulp of nonchalance*
*a tangled streak*
*of summer hair*

*running on the hot heat wave*
*rising up*
*sand stuck between toes*
*painted pink laugh*

*moonlight floating*
*on a wave of*
*caramel salt*
*crushed beneath*
*icy drops of a beach shower*

the car tar race of pavement
a child's face pressed to the glass
a ditch full of tall weeds
calling her name
swaying proud in the wind
snow drift melt

embedded memory of blue uniforms
a badge of pride
plucking fuzz with nervous fingers
listening to the howl of
the cold lost path
socks wet in sneakers
shiver

even as the wind
spun gold out of sand's last rock

the light drifts up
waking your curled body
and for a moment
we are one.

Darlene shares some thoughts about her poem and why she chose the accompanying photograph: "My grandmother was Cree Indian, and she grew up on the sand ridges above the lake. She always lived around the lake, and our histories are entwined in the memories of water lapping on sand, fishing, swimming and growing up. Her house was next door to our house, and my childhood and teen years were spent listening to her stories and wandering the beaches and rocky woodlands of that lake. I no longer live there, and she died of cancer when I was pregnant with my son, but every time we travel back to my hometown, we go to the lake and I remember. This photo was taken one summer weekend when I took my husband and son home to the water of my childhood. Photos of my family members—of our past—take me back to a specific memory in time, but it is the photos of the landscape of my home that fill me with the emotional memories of myself and those I love."

# ARTIST ILLUMINATION
## INTERVIEW WITH DARLENE KREUTZER

Here is a glimpse into how Darlene sees herself.

**Who are you?**
*a grown woman in pigtails,*
*moving lightly through the joyous bubble,*
*eyes dancing light*
*i twirl and dance*
*and live in a moment that doesn't need to create*
*anything more than the breath of that second.*
*there is no memory*
*because pure moments cannot be defined*
*by the words of our limitation,*
*creation.*

**Who or what inspires you?**
I always have a hard time with this question as I have been, and continue to be, deeply inspired by so many different authors, books, poems, songs and blogs. To speak of just a few seems as though I am excluding so many others, and, to be honest, I rarely read or see something that doesn't deeply inspire me. I was introduced to Natalie Goldberg's books in my first years of university, and her words continue to inspire me today. Her book *Writing Down the Bones* is one that I continue to come back to on a regular basis.

**How do you nurture yourself?**
I nurture myself with comfort. This has looked different for me at different stages of my life, but they are always solitary activities. Lately, it's solitary walks with one of my cameras allowing myself to connect to the natural world; working in my garden allows my heartbeat to combine with the beat of earth's life; making steaming pots of simmering soup; and filling my soul with reading and movies and sketching and playing with paint.

DARLENE'S RESPONSE TO "WHO ARE YOU?"

**How did you find your creative voice?**
I feel like I have always had a creative voice, and as I move through the paths of my journey, my creative voice changes and grows, expands and sometimes contracts into hiding. I grew up very poor, and at a very early age, I saw and experienced some ugly parts of humanity, but that was balanced by a lovely and hopeful family who encouraged me to have my own voice and to explore my creativity. I often feel that I have always walked with one foot in the shadows and one foot in the light, and being creative has enabled me to marry the two in a way that allows me to create a life that makes me smile.

## ON THE PAGE:
# THE SENSES OF A MEMORY

The senses can be an informative and enlightening guide as you explore memories from yesterday or twenty years ago.

**TASK:** Choose a memory or image from your childhood, and use the senses as a tool to capture this memory.

**NOTES:** The memory might be specific, such as Christmas morning 1985, or more broad, such as time spent at your grandparents' farm or riding your bike around your neighborhood when you were eight. You might want to choose one sense to work with or explore the senses one right after the other as you did in the "Senses of This Moment" exercise. You could also explore a specific sense in a general way, such as remembering the textures of your aunt's living room or listening to the sounds of an afternoon in the city with your father.

**EXAMPLE:** Here are some thoughts I jotted down as I reflected on the sounds of the times I spent with my grandmother:

*Her voice says "come on" as she insists we walk around her yard right after breakfast.*
*The water rushes as soap is squirted and dishes slide, then knock together.*
*Flip-flops clop toward the indoor pool and then the joy of laughter when we see we have it all to ourselves.*
*The guest room door creaks as she peeks to see if I am awake yet.*
*The brush solidly placed on the vanity when she finishes brushing her hair.*
*The head-back-mouth-open laughter as she watches my brother and me slide down the backyard hill in our green sleds.*
*The word "hello" just after my grandfather hands her the phone.*

## ON THE PAGE:
# IMAGINING THEIR WORLD

As you think about the people who came before you, you might find yourself in the midst of a personal history lesson that takes you to the library, the Internet or a more personal resource, such as a relative willing to share her stories, to find out even more about where you come from.

**TASK:** Imagine the life of those who came before you, and capture this image through the senses and words.

**NOTES:** Ponder the pieces you know about your parents' parents and their family members. Maybe you know that your great-grandmother moved from Pennsylvania to Nebraska by covered wagon. Perhaps your father has told you stories of childhood hours spent with his grandmother as she talked about life at the turn of the century. You could also bring your own experiences in and compare them to the past. For example, maybe your mother taught you to knit and you can imagine her learning from her great-grandmother, just as you learned from her.

**EXAMPLE:** Photography can be a wonderful clue to use with this exercise. Recently, I uncovered a photo of the farm where my grandmother grew up (a place that I never visited), and in the background of the photo, I can see there are people in the yard. Looking closer, I can see five sisters of this family standing together getting their picture taken. As I looked at this photo, I wrote some notes that I will use as the basis for a poem. Here are just a few sentences from these notes:

*These women are now wives and mothers, but in this moment, they stand together again as sisters. The photo is black and white, but I see the colors of this summer day in the middle of Indiana. The deep green of the towering maple against the blue sky, the thirsty grass of the yard that surrounds them, the needing-another-coat-of-white-paint farmhouse.*

# Unearthing Your Artistic Adventurer

Now we look at how these whispers and images of our past influence the art we create. As I mentioned earlier in this chapter, my art and writing is greatly influenced by reflecting on people who lived before me. Through the journey of losing loved ones, I have grown to cherish the letters to and from them, photographs of the people I knew and those relatives I did not and the treasures (now vintage) that lived in their homes. Let's look at how shining our flashlight on the past can teach us about what we create.

ARTWORK BY LIZ LAMOREUX

Last fall, my friend Kelly Rae Roberts invited me to join her for an afternoon of creativity and painting. I brought a canvas and a random packet of papers from previous workshops I had attended. When I began to pull out my art supplies, I realized the paper I had grabbed was full of photocopies of letters and photographs from my past. With Kelly's guidance here and there while we worked side by side, I created the piece you see here.

I started with simply getting the collage elements I wanted onto the canvas without worrying too much about placement, and then I applied paint using a roller. As I created this piece, I had to push aside thoughts like, "I want to be able to read the entire letter" and "I want to be able to see their faces" in order to see the photos and letters as a background for the collage I was creating. Adding color pushed me to decide which parts of the background were most important to me, and you can still see them through the paint. As we were working, I told Kelly I wanted to add some sort of writing, and she suggested stamping the text. The phrase "rooted in love" kept swirling in my mind while I was working, so I added it in bold black letters.

The idea of bringing the visual pieces of the past into what we create honors our past while revealing where we have been and how it has shaped us. You can combine this with the senses investigations you did in this chapter to pull together objects that represent your writing and memories.

Contributor Annie Lockhart's assemblage is created with treasures that represent pieces of her past. Using an old book cover as a canvas, Annie brought together nature elements and several vintage elements including various fiber and sewing bits, millinery, a compass and a key, among other items. For Annie, creating from the past invites a sense of power from the lessons learned and wisdom gathered over one's life. The layers that you can see in her assemblage pieces represent the internal layers of her life experiences that have brought her to this moment.

Annie also feels there is a thread of memories that exist in many of her pieces. She explained that she knows it is there, but others might not realize these hidden truths. Assemblage is a way to create without words while still tucking those memories into the layers of the piece.

In the next chapter, we will look at what we gather to us—what we are drawn to—as another layer of insight into where we are on our path. Annie's grandmothers were both collectors, and she has followed in their footsteps. In high school, her drawing teacher had her arrange the still lifes the class would draw. This invited her to see ways to put her collections into stories of light, shadow and texture, which influences her today.

## Tools for the Journey:
### Assemblage Tips from Annie

FIND SOMETHING TO BE THE "BONES" OF THE PIECE: In Annie's piece, she used a vintage book cover. Think about other options such as scraps of wood, a lampshade, an old piece of china, fabric and so on.

ADHERING MEDIUMS: Wire is Annie's favorite "tool." The practical reason is that unlike glue, you don't have to wait for it to dry; a more artistic reason is that it adds texture. She also uses clear silicone, upholstery tacks, hooks, waxed linen and an assortment of fixatives.

THINK OF FOUND OBJECTS AS YOUR WORDS: You can create an assemblage from a poem you wrote, using gathered objects to stand in for your actual poetry.

CONSIDER THIS EXERCISE: Gather potential assemblage items in a box, varying the items by design elements such as color, scale, texture and repetition. Then, create an assemblage from these items.

WORK WITH WHAT YOU HAVE: Push yourself to figure out how to attach things: Let the experience of creating in the third-dimension flow. It is okay if things look a bit haphazard because then they look like they have been that way for years.

REMEMBER THAT YOUR WORK CAN GROW AS YOU CHANGE: Days or even years later you might want to change or add something.

ARTWORK BY ANNIE LOCKHART

## IN THE STUDIO:
# AN EXPRESSION OF THE PAST

Do you already use personal photos and ephemera in your artwork? If you do, examine why you are drawn to do so. If you haven't directly explored creating with photos and other items from your past, spend some time with these pieces in your creative space.

**TASK:** Gather the photos (and any other pieces of the past such as letters) you explored earlier in this chapter. Spend some time asking yourself questions about the message these photos might have for you. What can you learn from these moments captured from your past? Think about how you can honor these lessons and truths in a mixed-media creation. Use copies of old photos, letters and other ephemera to create a collage (or another piece of art).

**NOTES:** You might want to create a collage as I did in the "Rooted" example on page 43. Consider using acrylic or watercolor paint, your sewing machine or other mediums. Collages do not always have to be limited to paper and paint. If you decide to use the photos and letters, be sure to use copies because you may want to revisit them in the future minus the paint and other mediums that could obscure them. I used a combination of photocopies and photos printed out with my ink-jet printer, and the ink did not "run" when I brushed gel medium over them.

## IN THE STUDIO:
# BRINGING IN THE SENSES

Invite the senses into your studio to see what they reveal to you.

**TASK:** Using the photography and poetry senses exercises that you explored in this chapter, incorporate the senses into your artwork and into the actual experience of creating it.

**NOTES:** Push yourself to move past the idea that the senses have to be represented visually. For example, you could decide to create outdoors to notice how the sounds of nature or the city influence what you create. You might want to bring smells, such as flowers or food, into your studio space and focus on your sense of smell while you are creating. For the artwork itself, you might want to think about how you can add more texture as Annie does in her three-dimensional assemblage pieces. You might want to add photographs that stimulate the senses by creating associations.

# ARTIST ILLUMINATION
## INTERVIEW WITH ANNIE LOCKHART

Here is a glimpse into how Annie sees herself.

### Who are you?

*I am like a silver transparency catching the light*
*I am like a mellow shadow tracing lines of richness*
*I am like a dreamy song tattered in laughing colors*
*I am like a season of changing choices written in red*
*I am like a nourishing anchor dancing in the wind*
*I am like a tangible boundary in unknown territory*
*I am like a subtle stone of strength in the riverbed*
*I am like a blend of anticipation learning from the unexpected*

### Who or what inspires you?

My inward journey began so long ago, and it seems that it's a never-ending one, one that I try desperately to keep my heart open to whenever someone new crosses my path. There are so many individuals that touch my life—who have inspired me along the way. My grandmother for one has been an immeasurable source of strength and inspiration to me. She's hard to top, but several years ago, I, along with thousands of others, felt the tug of *The Call* by Oriah Mountain Dreamer. I'm also inspired by the poem "Desiderata" by Max Ehrmann, as well as any work by Henry David Thoreau. I am also a fan of children's books because they keep me seeing life from a child's eye!

### How do you nurture yourself?

Whenever I need to nurture myself, I turn to nature! Anything to do with stepping out into the elements has always had a healing effect on me—water being my number one choice—so I get to the ocean as often as I can. I am humbled beyond belief in her presence and power. I feel part of the universe—connected to love—when I choose to open these gifts of wonderment. Photographing nature is something that I do for myself as well. Looking through the viewfinder nudges me to see even the simplest weeds in a new light.

### How did you find your creative voice?

I feel lucky that my creative voice actually found *me* at a very early age. I've not ever known a time when I didn't need or want to create. Having a creative grandmother helped and having a mother who was not creative also helped. (I mean that in a good way!) Those early observations laid a ground-work for how I wanted to live. I'm finding that listening to (and acting upon) your creative voice is a choice. There were times that I didn't want to listen to what it was saying. My critic stepped in many times to discourage me, but creativity is a wonderfully funny thing—it really can take on its own life. I am, by nature, an all-or-nothing kind of gal. When I jump into something, I sometimes have blinders on to the world around me—not always good, such as when I was raising five small children! I'm finding that choosing to live a cre-ative life is a lesson of balance. I'm still working on this balance.

ANNIE'S RESPONSE TO "WHO ARE YOU?"

## *Delving Into the Quiet:*

# THE CHILD WHO IS YOU

As you sift through the photos of your past, find a photo of yourself as a child. Choose a photo that you like. (I chose this young photo of me—so very happy at the ocean—as opposed to the fifth-grade class photos I came across that suggested bangs I might have cut myself.) If you are having trouble with this, you might need to call in another person for support. For example, I explained this exercise to my aunt while we were looking through family photos, and I uncovered one of her that I love. She said that she never likes photos of herself as a child because someone once made fun of her smile. I explained what I saw when I looked at the photo (a beautiful, shy little girl with the world waiting for her), which pushed her to see herself in a different way.

After you choose your photo, spend some time writing about what you see when you look it. You might take just a few minutes to do this or journal on this topic for a while. Perhaps use a phrase like "I see you there . . ." and describe what you see. See where your memories take you. Remember how the world was waiting for you.

Then, find a place in your home where you can place your photo and see it daily. I leaned mine against the bathroom mirror. (My husband just smiles at me whenever I do this sort of thing.) Each day, greet that child who is you and remember how she or he is still a part of who you are. You might even want to start a collection of little treasures that represent pieces of your childhood and put them near your photo. I have shells I collected with my grandmother and a candle I light every now and then in remembrance of these really good memories at the beach with my family.

# CHAPTER 3: *I gather*

In this chapter, we look at what we gather to us— what we are drawn to repeatedly in our worlds. If we open our eyes and minds to reflect on how we spend our days, what fills the world we inhabit, what we see over and over again, we gain insight into who we are in this moment, in the days before today. We can then determine who it is we want to be tomorrow.

Let's begin by focusing on the broader idea of what you gather to you. When you look at the world around you, what textures do you see? How does the world you inhabit feel when you reach out to touch it? What sounds do you notice? What pulls you in? Are you pulled to the sea, the woods, the quiet? Do you seek time with others or solitude?

Even though my days are often filled with solitary stillness because I work from home, I am drawn to crashing waves and hours spent with sand beneath my feet as I fill my pockets with shells and sea glass. I picture myself taking "photo-walks" around the world with my friends as we capture the smells and textures of what it means to live, really live inside the city, on the coast, in the woods. I daydream about afternoons spent on patchwork quilts that tell the stories of lives lived before me, surrounded by books filled with poems and a journal at the ready. Even if each day is not filled with moments spent in these places, I gather these places, colors, textures to me as I walk on my path and seek time when I can find my way toward them.

Perhaps you, too, daydream of places that call your name, places you hope to spend your days. Where are these destinations that call you? What textures and sounds in your world are you drawn to?

Now let's focus on what you gather to you in your home. When you walk into your house, what do you see? Are you surrounding yourself with things that matter to you (and others who live with you)? What feelings does your sacred space of home invite? Spend time walking through your home and notice. What words come to mind when you look closely at each room, corner, wall?

When I think of home, I imagine soft, cozy spaces for conversation, play, creating. I see bowls filled with shells, jars of vintage buttons, handmade tables and comfortable chairs. I see the colors discovered when one realizes that spring is rejoicing in all her beauty. I do not see clutter in this home in my mind, yet I do see a place that feels lived in. I am currently on a quest to

live this image into reality as I work through letting go of "things" that don't hold meaning for my little family.

In this chapter, you examine what surrounds you and what you decide to surround yourself with literally, such as the items in your home, and figuratively, such as what you are drawn to in nature, during your weekends and so on. Through words and photography, you will explore the colors, the textures, the feelings, the views, the possibilities that make up where you live, where you work, where you are on your path. Then, you'll look at how you can add these observations to your artwork.

# Seeking Light and Shadow

When you capture the world around you with a camera, you begin to literally see the pieces that "catch your eye." When you push yourself to see the little things, the different angles, the textures, the colors, how a moment invites you to feel, patterns emerge. Perhaps you already know what you are drawn to when you stand behind your lens. Maybe you have been using your camera exclusively for family photos until now. Wherever you are as a photographer, this section is a little push to see your world with your eyes wide open, to see the nuances of a moment, of your life.

# PHOTOGRAPHY EXCURSION:
# ON THE GROUND

We begin with an exercise to push you to see your world from a new angle.

**TASK:** Put your camera on the ground to capture the world from an ant's view. You can also lean down toward the ground to snap a photo, but don't point your camera toward the ground; instead, face the lens toward the horizon. Consider using your timer and becoming a part of the photograph.

**NOTES:** If you don't want to get your camera dirty, bring a towel or some other prop to put under your camera to protect it. I often take photos from the ground while visiting water. I am careful, but a rogue wave has been known to surprise me, so be aware of how you might need to protect your camera in your chosen location.

**EXAMPLE:** The following photos capture places in my world that I love to visit, from an angle I would not see if I was walking with my eyes simply facing forward. Putting the camera on the ground gives me a view that somehow captures the feelings of these places I love.

PHOTO BY LIZ LAMOREUX

For the last few years, I have been taking a series of "from the ground" photos when I visit the water. This one was taken on the Oregon Coast at that special time before sunset when the light dances. I put the camera right on the ground and clicked.

I had a free afternoon while attending Squam Art Workshops in New Hampshire. After spending time reflecting on my journey of finding my way to feeling more grounded in my life, I captured this photo to express the joy I feel when I find my feet firmly beneath me.

**PHOTOS BY LIZ LAMOREUX**

This photo captures a unique view of the front porch of my grandparents' home. I boosted the color with a digital photo processing program and added a slight frame of black to enhance the photo's focus.

The trees of the Pacific Northwest seem so wise as they stand tall and surround us. At Point Defiance Park in my town, I found myself face-to-face with this one and decided to capture an angle I don't usually see while also taking a self-portrait with my camera's timer.

Even though almost sixty years separates our ages, my great-aunt and I spend many afternoons together chatting and laughing. She teaches me about gardening, and every time we visit, we walk into her backyard so she can show me what she has been up to. This photo of her yard was taken during one of these backyard excursions.

Let's begin to look more closely and examine the colors, senses, feel and views of your world. We will examine these things by pushing ourselves to not just look at "what you see in your home" but instead to turn this idea on its head into something like "seek the sounds of your evening."

To illustrate this, I asked two of my favorite photographers to answer some questions through photographs about how they seek the nuances, the textures, the sounds of where they are on their journey.

Contributing artist Susannah Conway answers the question, "What nourishes you?" in the following Polaroid photographs.

As you look at Susannah's photos, think about how her photographs answer this question in a richer way than a list of words might. (In this case the words would be: her bed, words, journaling, lunch with friends, nature, photography.) As I look at these photos, I want to step into them. The surfaces, patterns, smells, light and insights into Susannah's world pull the viewer right in.

## Tools for the Journey:
### Photos in an Instant

During the past few years, the artistic online community appears to be in the midst of a fascination with instant photos. From Polaroids to Fuji Instax cameras, photographers and bloggers are enjoying the vintage feel of instant film. With this medium, you experience instant gratification as the film develops before your eyes. I have several artist friends who enjoy using instant cameras because they find it easy to add the photos directly to art journals and other creative projects. Although at the time of this writing, Polaroid has stopped making instant film, in 2010, The Impossible Project began producing instant film to use with Polaroid cameras.

PHOTOS BY SUSANNAH CONWAY

Her answers to the question: What nourishes you?

PHOTOS BY SUSANNAH CONWAY

Her answers to the question: What nourishes you?

# ARTIST ILLUMINATION
## INTERVIEW WITH SUSANNAH CONWAY

Here is a glimpse into how Susannah sees herself.

**Who are you?**

*I am . . .*
*. . . a memory catcher*
*a seer*
*a storyteller*
*a wide ocean*
*an explorer*
*a seeker of solitude*
*a work in progress*

**Who or what inspires you?**

Stephanie Ericsson's book, *Companion Through the Darkness*, comforted me when I didn't think I could carry on. By sharing her truth she not only helped me through my grief, but she also inspired me to begin telling my own story.

**How do you nurture yourself?**

I let myself sink into the words of others—poetry, fiction and creative nonfiction. I allow myself to sleep in on the weekends and eat whatever my body craves. I drink lots of water; I treat my skin respectfully. Music accompanies me throughout my day; a camera and journal are always close at hand. I say no when I don't want to do something; I say yes when it feels right.

**How did you find your creative voice?**

Honestly? Through trial and error, slowly, over the years. By trying different things and running with the successes while chalking up the failures. By listening intently to what my heart was telling me. By being incredibly honest and telling my story.

SUSANNAH'S RESPONSE TO "WHO ARE YOU?"

Let's look at another artist's photography responses to several questions. The details of Susan Tuttle's photos that answer the question "What do you see when you open your eyes and really look" push me to want to investigate the art of taking close-up photographs (macrophotography) to see more details of the world around me. Looking at these two photos, you can almost feel the contrasting textures of the insect and the mushroom. As you look as Susan's answer to "What are the sounds of the moment," can you hear the giggles, splashing, dripping? Do the "visual sounds" of this photo echo moments from your own childhood?

What nourishes you?

What do you see when you open your eyes and really look?

What do you see when you open your eyes and really look?

What are the sounds of this moment?

# BEHIND THE LENS:
# SEEING WITH EYES WIDE OPEN

Let's continue to explore how a photo can be an intriguing, thought-provoking answer to a question.

**TASK:** Answer the following questions in photos:
What color is your morning?
What are the shapes of your day?
What are the smells of your evening?
What are the textures of your weekend?
What are the sounds of this moment?
What nourishes you?
What do you see when you open your eyes and really look?

**NOTES:** Perhaps you will want to take a series of photos that answer each question. I can imagine spending an entire month trying to capture the sounds of one moment in a day. Consider looking through photos you have already taken to see how you captured the answers to these questions. Reflect on similar questions that push you to look, and then look closer at your world.

As you examine Susannah's and Susan's photos, think about how you can capture what you gather to you in your life through photos. Think about the sounds that bring you joy and how you can photograph those sounds. Reflect on the senses exercises from Chapter 2. Think about how the senses relate to this next layer of self-portraiture.

# Revealing the Poet Within

In this chapter, we look at what we discover and collect on our journey, literally and in more intangible ways. In doing this, we gain insight into who we are and who we want to be. When we then put these observations into words, perhaps through poems or other writing, we push ourselves to find clues and claim the truths within our thoughts that become tangible on paper.

# FOLLOW YOUR MIND'S STREAM

As we begin the writing exploration in this chapter, let's start with another exercise to add to your creative toolbox.

**TASK:** In this exercise, you will write in your stream-of-consciousness voice for ten minutes. This means you will simply write whatever your mind tosses at you—regardless of whether or not it seems to make sense—and fill up a few pages in your journal or on your computer.

**NOTES:** It is helpful to set a timer before you begin this exercise so that you aren't distracted by looking at a clock. Don't pick up your pencil or stop typing even if you are simply repeatedly writing, "I really don't want to do this." Having this simple freewriting exercise in your arsenal is so helpful when you are stuck creatively and need to release yourself from your thoughts. Consider other freewriting practices:

- Begin your writing with a question and write all that comes up as you answer that question for ten minutes.

- Write a certain number of pages in your journal each morning or evening for a few weeks. Notice how you feel after your brain lets go before your day begins or as it ends.

- If something in your life is challenging you, spend a set amount of time writing about this to listen to your own inner wisdom.

**Excavator's Notebook:**
Poetry Assumptions

Answer this question: What assumptions do you have about poetry? Write them all down. The good, the bad, the ugly—all should be aired here.

When I began to write poetry as part of my personal writing practice, I would sometimes feel trapped in the need to have a finished poem. I would get stuck with just a line or two, unable to remember why I wanted to even write the poem in the first place. Somewhere along the way, I had decided that poetry had to be long and feel finished and simply be "good," and this stifled my writing for a while.

To pull myself out of this rut, I started writing quick poems that were much shorter, simplified versions of the stream-of-consciousness writing we looked at in the previous exercise. As these short poems became a regular writing exercise for me, I began to call these short writings "poem notes." Poem notes can be: notes for a poem you hope to write one day, short phrases, questions, the beginning lines of a poem. When I approach poetry writing as writing a poem note, I often find myself in the middle of a finished poem.

You might already be familiar with the idea of poem notes. Perhaps you write them on your blog when you capture a moment with just a few words. Maybe you are comfortable in the world of poetry and write in short poem form (such as haikus and cinquains) already. On the other hand, you might be thinking, "What in the world is a poem note, really?" The following are some examples.

Three poem notes from contributing artist Judy Wise:

April 19, 2009
*insomnia last night*
*hard work*
*chasing ideas*
*across the vast prairie*
*on a white horse*
*under burning stars*

August 29, 2009
*quiet mornings*
*nourish me*
*pencil*
*journal*
*coffee*
*unearthing*
*my own*
*slow*
*rhythm*

Sept. 9, 2009
*last night I slashed the page with paint*
*letting my frustrations out*
*making a muddy, incoherent mess*
*layer upon layer*
*until at last glimmers of beauty*
*presented themselves*
*calming my restive spirit*
*islands*
*in an ocean of chaos*

This is a poem note I wrote early in the morning on New Year's Eve 2009:

*Today,*
*I am leaning in toward self-care and hope*
*Twisting inside doubt*
*Twirling through all that love creates*
*Sitting still beneath the wisdom of the teachers*
*who surround me*

Kelly Barton answers the question, "What color is your morning?" in this poem note:

*feet padding across the cool floor,*
*deep shadows billowing against*
*the stairway walls. eyes gaze, a*
*warm ball rests upon the neighboring*
*rooftop.*

*eyes close as the morning cup is filled*
*with memories of the days, waking up*
*with melba. the toast warm with melting*
*butter and honey. dark coffee filtering*
*through the halls.*

*feet padding across the cool floor. looking*
*for that spot where a moment of calm can be*
*found. waiting for the crazy to begin.*

Additionally, you might have already noticed that each contributing artist is answering the question "Who are you?" in a poem note in the Artist Illuminations throughout the book.

When you notice what you gather to you in your world and put these observations into words, you can find the patterns and the nuances, and you can continue to see where you are on your path.

## ON THE PAGE:
# PRACTICE POEM FROM NOTHING

As you find your way to discovering this moment, you just might find your way to a poem.

**TASK:** Describe this moment in a poem note.

**NOTES:** Imagine you are writing a quick note to a friend about this moment. Push yourself to bring in the senses as you create an image of where you are, what you hear and so on in just a few lines. You can also use a different moment from this day. Maybe you noticed the buds on the dogwood this morning, or just for a second, maybe your child's laughter pulled you away from the bills you were paying. Describe moments like these in a few short lines.

## ON THE PAGE:
# WORDS THAT CAPTURE YOUR WORLD

Let's revisit a few questions to examine the images and textures of your world, but this time, you will answer "in poem."

**TASK:** Answer the following questions in poem notes:
What color is your morning?
What are the shapes of your day?
What are the smells of your evening?
What are the textures of your weekend?
What are the sounds of this moment?
What nourishes you?
What do you see when you open your eyes and really look?

**NOTES:** You might want to answer with a list of words. Perhaps you will write in short paragraphs or simple phrases stacked on top of one another. Think about other questions like these that will push you to look closer at the images, at the senses that surround you.

# Unearthing Your
# Artistic Adventurer

In this section, we will examine the idea that what we collect and gather on our journey will often show up in the art we create. As a result, this artwork becomes another self-portrait, even when we don't set out to label it as such.

Throughout this book, each contributing artist's work illustrates the idea that what we gather to us appears in our work. I can imagine Annie Lockhart's studio filled with vintage keys, letters and fabric that sits beside collections of shells, buttons and ribbon. I can see bright, happy colors in the form of patterned paper, paint and photographs in Kelly Barton's space. I imagine Judy Wise surrounded by her journals, art supplies and talismans from her travels.

If you walked into my home today, you would soon see that I am drawn to paintings and mixed-media pieces that have figures and faces—especially those of women. When I first began to play with paint, I simply had fun swirling colors together and adding paper and words. Then, I decided I needed to figure out how to "make a girl" with paint. But I had no experience drawing or painting faces, and the negative inner dialogue that came up when I attempted it pushed me away from wanting to paint at all. I spent months almost frozen creatively because of this need to "paint a girl." Somehow I had arrived at the conclusion that to be an artist I must be able to paint a girl.

During this time, I was gifted a sewing machine. My mother came for a visit, and we spent the weekend playing with fabric. I revisited the little seamstress I had been twenty years before when I first learned to sew. However, I didn't consider this playing with fabric to be art. Even as I began to gather vintage buttons, old spools of thread and vintage fabric and started to draft my own patterns and play with patchwork, I did not recognize how I was finding my inner fabric artist. One day, while sewing one of my poems to a piece of linen that would become part of a set of prayer flags, I suddenly started laughing as I realized the joy I was experiencing. I was finding my creative voice. All it had taken was beginning to play with the very things that I was drawn to surround myself with.

**Excavator's Notebook:**
Finding Your Voice

Look inward to ask yourself if you are pushing your creative journey in a direction that doesn't fit who you really are. Are you spending time wishing you could paint like someone else instead of finding your own voice?

Please know that I am not suggesting that you shouldn't try to create what you feel called to. This is why we take workshops from artists we admire, to learn from them and, as artist Kelly Rae Roberts says, "step into their style."

In my example, I was stuck because I was insisting that being an artist had to look like something specific. A few years later, I found myself in a class with Judy Wise where she gently led me to create my first painted face. I loved every second of that workshop. But, I needed the years prior to it where I had begun to find my own voice before I could revisit painting.

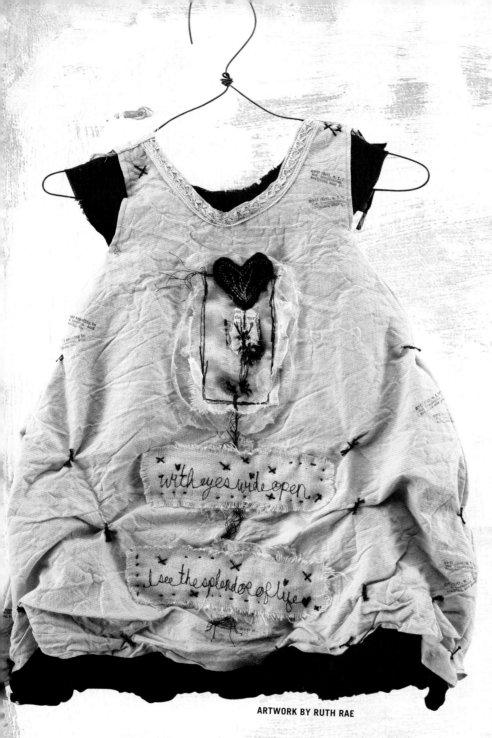

**ARTWORK BY RUTH RAE**

Let's revisit the questions we have examined in the poetry and photography sections of this chapter:

*What color is your morning?*
*What are the shapes of your day?*
*What are the smells of your evening?*
*What are the textures of your weekend?*
*What are the sounds of this moment?*
*What nourishes you?*
*What do you see when you open your eyes and really look?*

Can you imagine ways to bring in the answers you found through photography and poetry into your artwork? When we do a bit of investigative work like this before we create, our artwork becomes another tangible way to see where and who we are.

I asked contributing artist Ruth Rae to write a poem note response to one of these questions and then use that poem note in a piece of art. If you are familiar with Ruth's art, you know that she often uses lines from poetry in her beautifully detailed, mixed-media fiber creations. In this piece, Ruth has combined linen, felt, thread and other fiber to create a gorgeous dress that gently holds her words. Her poem note, a response to the question "What do you see when you open your eyes and really look?" reads:

*with eyes wide open*
*I see the splendor of life*

# ARTIST ILLUMINATION
## INTERVIEW WITH RUTH RAE

Here is a glimpse into how Ruth sees herself.

**Who are you?**

*I live this abundant life filled with an inner confidence.
I am courageously transforming as I journey forward
with passion.
I breathe my existence . . .
I am forever me.*

**Who or what inspires you?**

Poetry and the written word have always
had a tremendous influence on me throughout my life. Words somehow feed a vast
amount of my creativity. I have received
great influences from the Bible, Rumi, Khalil
Gibran, ee cummings, Helen Keller and
Edgar Allan Poe.

**How do you nurture yourself?**

Allowing myself the freedom to grow and
change without reservation and treating
myself with the same kindness and compassion that I treat others is the best way that I
know how to nurture my soul.

**How did you find your creative voice?**

A visceral girl at heart, my creative voice was
obtained through intuition rather than from
reasoning or observation. I am completely
intoxicated with color and texture and allow
myself to freely explore all the possibilities
of play when I create.

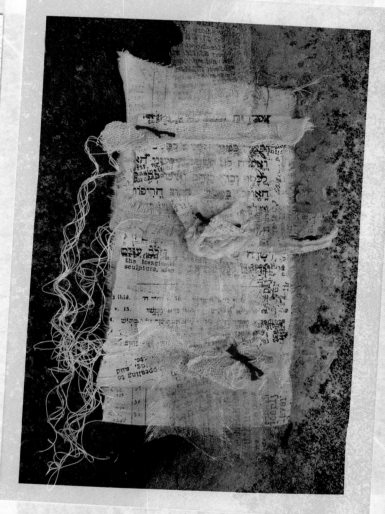

RUTH'S RESPOSE TO "WHO ARE YOU?"

## IN THE STUDIO:
# CREATING WITH WHAT WE GATHER

Again, as you revisit the questions in this chapter, look at how your answers can influence the mediums with which you create and what you are drawn to express through your art.

**TASK:** Use your answers to questions in this chapter as a creative prompt.

**NOTES:** Think about what you collect and what you are drawn to and how these things appear in your artwork. If it feels as though they do not appear, push yourself to create your next piece of art using the prompt of your answers to the questions in this chapter.

**EXAMPLE:** A fabric journal I created was inspired by my poem note response to the question, "What are the textures of your weekend?" and appears on page 129. My poem note reads:

*Pink buttons disguised as flowers*
*Linen handkerchiefs trimmed by hand*
*The perfect discarded patchworked square*
*Words twirling to find a spot to land*
*Worn by living piles of rocks, shells*
*These are pieces of the texture that is this life,*
*That is my life.*

With this poem note as my prompt, I decided to create a journal that houses some of my poetry. In addition to sewing my poem right onto the cover, I also used some of my favorite things—fabric, vintage sewing elements and buttons—to remind myself that using the things I love in my studio pushes me to continue to hear my creative voice.

## IN THE STUDIO:
# POETRY + ART = A VERY GOOD THING

What would happen if you brought poetry into your studio? Let's find out.

**TASK:** Add a poem note to your next mixed-media creation.

**NOTES:** Perhaps you will want to use one of the poem notes you wrote in the previous poetry exercise. Maybe you will want to create something new to add to your piece. Consider the following:

• If you are a fabric artist, consider adding words with embroidery or free-motion quilting or literally sewing your poem that's on a piece of paper onto your fabric.
• If you are working with collage or paint, think about a space where your text can be read. Maybe you will want to leave a less busy space specifically where the text can appear with few distractions (such as in the corner of your collage). Perhaps you will want to add the text to the background so only you know what it says, or you might write the words around a collage element, such as adding text inside a figure/face/body, and so on.

# *Delving Into the Quiet:*

## CREATING AN ALTAR

During my training as a yoga teacher, I learned about the idea of creating a personal space set aside just for you in your home. You might already have a place where you often read, write, meditate, create. Whether you have your own space or haven't yet claimed even a small space as your own, you can create a personal altar that represents pieces of what you gather to you and what is important to you. There are many theories and reasons behind altars, but my focus is more on creating a space where you can be reminded to take a deep breath and feel grounded in your life.

On a side table in our family room, I have set up an altar space that holds a few photos that are important to me. I then gathered and added treasures that represent my spiritual views. I wanted nature to be a part of this space, so I added a few rocks I've found on my beach walks and a feather found at a park near our home. Also, the altar holds a few shells from my grandmother's collection, sea glass from a dear friend, a small rock from another friend and other gifts I have received that represent family and friends. I light a candle in this space when I want to remind myself of where I come from and where I am right now. I also send out blessings or thoughts to those who may need them and "bring" those people to my altar through photographs or other elements when it feels right to do so. In our home, we actually have several little altar spaces, but this one is the most personal to me. Other spaces are more like mini-altars with a candle at the center and then other items surrounding it.

Think about creating your own altar space. Consider photos, candles, nature elements and other things you might want to have in this space.

**PHOTO BY LIZ LAMOREUX**

67

# CHAPTER 4: *I see me*

Part of the journey inward includes noticing where we stand on our path. In Chapter 2, we looked at where we *have been*. In this chapter, we will look at where we *are*—where we stand in our lives. To do this, I believe we must examine our bodies, externally and internally, and take a look at how we see ourselves. We will dive into the inner dialogue that surfaces within, and look at the clues this chatter can give us.

A personal story about my own journey of looking inward and examining my body: I remember the day a few years ago when I sat quietly on my mat while my yoga students rested in savasana at the end of class. The music filled the room as I watched each of their bodies relax deeper into their mats, into themselves. I closed my eyes, and this thought entered my mind, "Not once do I think about how my body looks when I am teaching. Yet, so often outside of class, I find myself tripped up in negative thoughts about my body." I began to notice the thoughts that would emerge: I wish I looked like ___. Why can't they make cute clothes for women with curves? Are they going to like me when they realize I am not skinny?

After noticing these questions, I spent time writing about this contrast and what I know to be true about my body. Some of what I wrote a few years ago:

*I am grounded in my body. I feel the strength of my hips and thighs, even if I wish that they were smaller. I feel my body. I feel it. I stand in front of people and feel strong and capable. This is new, and this is huge—an unexpected gift. I move my body, stretching, opening, and I do not think about how I look as I move. I simply know I am moving the way I was meant to move. And maybe, just maybe, I can begin to see this as beautiful.*

I share this glimpse into pieces of my own relationship with my body as an invitation for you to begin to be honest with yourself about your own internal dialogue about your body and what it houses. We each have this inner chatter, sometimes positive and sometimes not so positive, and exploring this is a piece of excavating where we stand in our journeys.

## Excavator's Notebook:
### Your Body

*Spend a few moments writing about your body and the thoughts that arise when you simply think of your body, how it moves, how it feels, how you feel about it.*

This chapter gently pushes you to see the light that emanates from within you, the light that those who love you see, the light you might not always remember to notice. We will explore the world of self-portrait photography to capture this light. We will use these photos to then put into words what we see when we see ourselves. Then, we will look at how these words and photos can inspire the artwork we create.

## Delving Into the Quiet:
# FINDING THE BREATH

Find a comfortable way to sit and close your eyes. Take a few deep breaths.

Notice how your breath moves in your body until you feel as though you are only the inhalations and exhalations.

Then, find your center. Notice where it is.

Let your next inhalation begin at this center.

As you continue to breathe, try to let your mind rest in this center.

When a thought pulls you away from this center, notice the thought and then invite your mind to come back to rest in your breath, in this center.

**NOTES:** Try this for ten to twenty breath cycles. Over time, increase this to a few minutes. As you continue this practice, you will find that simply reconnecting to your breath with intention, even for just a breath or two, will bring you a sense of inner calm and peace.

# Seeking Light and Shadow

Exploring photos of our own bodies might seem daunting at first glance, but our goal in this section is to simply have fun. You are invited to let go of the assumptions you might have about what photos showing our bodies have to look like. Yes. Right now. Give yourself permission to let go of those assumptions.

# PHOTOGRAPHY EXCURSION:
# WHERE I STAND

Your photography excursion begins with an exercise that looks at how you are rooted to where you travel in your life by literally capturing where you stand on your path in a given moment.

**TASK:** Photograph the places where you stand in your life by taking photos of your feet and the ground beneath you.

**NOTES:** Play with camera placement. For example, put your camera on the ground. Capture your feet from above. If you have fun shoes, wear them! And if you dislike wearing shoes, don't wear any!

**EXAMPLE:** The following photographs represent the "Where I Stand" series I have been taking for a couple of years. By capturing my feet, instead of, for example, the place itself or my face/body in front of a scene, I am playing with the idea of being rooted in the moment when the photo is taken. As I experience the rhythms, adventures and twists of my life, this idea of staying rooted in the moment appeals to me. Also, it simply is fun to notice what shoes I am wearing, the colors of my clothes, the ground and so on, and to take in a moment in an unexpected way.

This photo was taken on the day I began writing *Inner Excavation*. When I came across these words, I had to snap this perfect reminder as I walked into unexplored territory.

**PHOTO BY LIZ LAMOREUX**

I attended the same grade school from kindergarten through the eighth grade. I hadn't been in the halls of that school in more than fifteen years, but when driving by during a visit home, we stopped. I stood tall in the atrium of this place that shaped who I am (wearing shoes I never would have been allowed to wear to school).

PHOTOS BY LIZ LAMOREUX

On a day in April, I stood in my grandparents' front yard for the last time. I leaned into all that they had taught me as I breathed in the scent of spring, my childhood and love.

The Pacific Northwest summer sun is the gift I long for in mid-February. On this summer day, a dear friend and I shared some secrets and hopes as we walked toward Puget Sound.

One of the goals of this book is to help you recognize the fun you can have taking self-portraits. Part of the joy of digital photography is that we can take so many photos and simply delete the ones we do not like or want. When I take self-portraits, I often take fifteen to twenty at a time. I want to capture different angles and emotions, but I also want a lot of photos to choose from as I usually share self-portrait photos on my blog. My internal critic has softened through these self-portrait exercises, but I still give myself permission to delete photos I do not like and share the few that I want to.

PHOTOS BY VIVIENNE MCMASTER

When I first saw one of contributing artist Vivienne McMaster's self-portrait photo sessions, I found myself literally exclaiming, "Wow!" out loud. This artist knows how to capture the many aspects of who she is with her self-portraits. Lucky for me, she had so much fun working on a series of photos for this book that I am able to include several examples for you to use as inspiration for your own self-portrait shoots.

The first series of Vivienne's photos echo the "Where I Stand" photos explored in the previous exercise. Vivienne placed her camera right on the railroad tracks and used her timer to capture these photos.

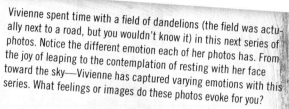

Vivienne spent time with a field of dandelions (the field was actually next to a road, but you wouldn't know it) in this next series of photos. Notice the different emotion each of her photos has. From the joy of leaping to the contemplation of resting with her face toward the sky—Vivienne has captured varying emotions with this series. What feelings or images do these photos evoke for you?

**PHOTOS BY
VIVIENNE MCMASTER**

74

PHOTOS BY VIVIENNE MCMASTER

In this last series, Vivienne captures light and movement as she stretches, twirls and reaches while the timer snaps the photo for her. What do you see underneath the movement shown in this series?

What I want you to notice most of all is the fun Vivienne clearly has when she takes these self-portraits. When I asked her about this, she said that the first few photos don't always convey this element, but as she begins to feel more comfortable, the fun emerges.

I also asked Vivienne why she is drawn to take self-portraits. She says that the logical reason is that they document stages of her life, but the true reason is that they have become her meditation. As she goes through the photos and finds the ones that speak to her the most, she has begun to see her authentic self—a self she doesn't always show. These portrait sessions have given her, in her words, "control of the way I view my own beauty."

75

# ARTIST ILLUMINATION
## INTERVIEW WITH VIVIENNE MCMASTER

Here is a glimpse into how Vivienne sees herself.

**Who are you?**
*I am the slowly exposing image of a Polaroid.
I am the upside down reflection of a dewdrop
on a petal.
I am the naiveté of a young child and the wise
energy of an old soul.
I am a wide smile, a belly laugh and a bear hug.
I am a heart worn on a sleeve and a girl full
of gratitude.*

**Who or what inspires you?**
A book of poetry by Hafiz and *Spilling Open*
by Sabrina Ward Harrison at my bedside.
My stereo blaring Ferron, Kinnie Starr and
Chris Pureka.
Daily images of my beloved photo-peers
on Flickr.
This is me—continually inspired.

VIVIENNE'S RESPONSE TO "WHO ARE YOU?"

**How do you nurture yourself?**
It's so important to me to live a nurtured
life. Photo walks in the botanical garden
near my house, savoring time alone, eat-
ing nutritious and delicious food, enjoying
beautiful music and curling up with my
cats are some of the ways that help me feel
nurtured. It also feels vital to me to create
every single day, be it painting, songwriting
or taking photos. It feeds me in a way nothing else does!

**How did you find your creative voice?**
Finding my creative voice is an adventure
of the best kind. I feel like I'm always
exploring it deeper. I think it's important
to learn from our creative community and
then push deeper to find a voice that is our
own. Trying new mediums, films, cameras
and techniques all push me further into
finding my uniqueness and authenticity.
I'm finding my creative voice through following those things that spark, energize
and endlessly excite me.

### BEHIND THE LENS:
# FINDING YOUR INNER LIGHT

Give yourself permission to find the light within you as you turn your camera toward you. Remember Vivienne's suggestion to recognize that you are in charge of this experience, which means you control how you see your own beauty.

**TASK:** Using your timer, take self-portraits of your body. Capture light, dancing, standing firmly on your own two feet. Look through Vivienne's photos for inspiration.

**NOTES:** Tools you might need for this exercise include:
• Camera with self-timer
• Remote (visit your local camera store to find one for your camera)
• Tripod
• Full camera battery
• Room on memory card
• Mirror
• Sense of humor
• Favorite clothes
• Props

Remember, we all have bad angles, and the beauty of digital photography is that you can take a lot of photos and feel free to delete the ones you don't like.

Vivienne puts her camera right on the ground when she takes her portraits. Sometimes I find a bench or some other flat surface to prop up mine. Other people I know always use a tripod and/or a remote, but I don't think that is always necessary because I like the freedom of just snapping away even if I only have my camera. Find what works for you.

# Revealing the Poet Within

In this section, we continue with an inward examination of our bodies; this time through poetry. As we look closer at ourselves, we will not just write about the body's physical form. We will also seek the clues that this exploration can give us about who we are and where we are on our journey. As we uncover these clues, we can begin to listen to our bodies and hearts and write down what they reveal to us.

# WORDS DISCOVERED:
# WHAT CONTRAST UNCOVERS

Here is another exercise to add to your writer's toolbox: the idea of using contrast in your writing. The use of opposites and contrast can be helpful because it causes the reader to pause and reflect on what you are conveying with these contrasts. At the same time, coming up with opposites pushes you, the writer, to be specific with your words.

**TASK:** Bring contrast into your writing by finishing the following phrases:

They see . . .
I am . . .
The world sees . . .
I feel . . .
They expect . . .
I wish . . .
They want . . .
I want . . .
I am . . .
I know . . .

**NOTES:** Come up with your own introductory phrases and finish them. Another idea is to finish beginning phrases like these but then delete the beginning phrases and look at the finished words that remain. Find a poem within those phrases. For example, you might write, "They see . . . someone always there to hold up the world. I am . . . the seed pirouetting to the ground." This might become a poem note that reads something like, "The seed pirouetting to the ground, unable to hold up the world, I seek roots."

As we turn now to reflect on how we can write about the body in a way that lets go of focusing only on the physical, we seek clues about this moment and where we are traveling on our path. This means we will let go of writing poems that simply describe how the body "looks" and delve deeper into what the body says, how the body feels, what the body knows.

How do we do this? Again, by inviting the inner chatter to rest while we investigate, we quiet the mind; we slow down and allow this writing to take on an almost meditative feel. When the negative thoughts appear, we can acknowledge them and then move on. I don't mean to make it sound easy. This is something that can take years of practice. However, just beginning this practice is a powerful tool.

Photography can be one tool to help with writing about the body. For example, photos taken by another person can reveal new layers to us. Note that I don't mean the family photos taken on your most recent vacation that invite you to remember how you wish you had lost that extra five pounds before getting on the plane. Rather, I mean someone capturing a photo that invites you to pause and really look at yourself in a new, positive way.

When I dance, I feel very at home in my body. When I came across a photo someone else had taken of me using my camera, I felt moved to write about the freedom I feel when dancing. The photo certainly isn't my favorite photo ever taken of me, yet it conveys the movement of dancing and the joy I experience when I move my body. I was truly lost in the dancing when this joy was captured so I began there when I sat down to write the following:

*I see her.*

*I see her grounded in her body as she moves across the floor, across the room, with arms twirling above her head. And her hips—those hips that shift and turn and twist to the beat of the song in the air. They twist and turn and she moves. How she moves to the music that seems to be part of her. It is as though she is directly connected to the boom ba boom of the beat of the sound in the air. She is directly connected to the soul of the singer and the rhythm as she moves and twists and twirls. Her long hair becomes another extension of the body as her hips circle and her knees bend and her toes point and her arms that once belonged to a ballerina remember what it feels like to stretch, as though they reach for the very moment when she first put on the ballet shoes and smiled that four-year-old girl's smile of joy.*

*I see her and marvel at how she lets go of the need to wonder what others are thinking or how she must look as her size sixteen body sinks inside the boom ba boom. She lets go of what others are thinking as she stretches her arms to either side and finds the rhythm with her fingertips and wrists as her hips rotate and her knees bend and her feet move quickly with purpose. Her feet move with a purpose that wraps the entire room in a circle that vibrates with joy.*

*I see her reflection as she twists and stretches and seems grounded in her body.*

*I see her and I see me.*

*I see me.*

*And I dance on.*

Giving voice to our bodies is another way to turn our awareness inward and away from focusing on just the physical appearance of our bodies. Imagine what your knees might say as they rest at the end of the day, how your shoulders feel as they hold the worries of your day, all that your eyes have seen and what they might want to tell you about their travels. Playing with this idea of giving voice to parts of our body or voice to what our body does (lungs that breathe, mind that processes, heart that beats and so on) can reveal clues to us about where we are on our journey. The following is a short poem I wrote giving voice to the space my breath creates around my heart.

*The space around my heart holds*
*The words of the women who came before me*
*The fear of a small child on the first day of school*
*The hope of a crocus blooming in February*
*The belief of a traveler who has seen*
*The truth of a weathered nugget of sea glass*

## ON THE PAGE:
# GIVING VOICE TO THE BODY

What is your body telling you? Listening is a practice of mindfulness, enabling you to pause and notice what you might normally ignore.

**TASK:** Choose a part of your body and give that body part a voice.

**NOTES:** Consider beginning your poem with a phrase similar to one of the following:
• My hands show . . .
• Her (His) eyes have seen . . .
• These legs have carried me . . .
• My heart beats the story of . . .

Your poem might be a few lines, or you might find yourself writing several paragraphs. Give yourself permission to just listen to what your body has to say.

## ON THE PAGE:
# SEEING YOUR LIGHT

This exercise is about celebrating what you see when you look at a photo of yourself.

**TASK:** Look at a photo of yourself (one that you like, perhaps one of the self-portraits you have taken from the photography exercise in this chapter or a photo someone else has taken of you) and write a poem to/about that photo.

**NOTES:** Consider beginning your poem with a phrase like "I see her/him" as I did in the previous example. Try to push yourself to look at the words that exist under any negative chatter that comes up. Going back to the example photo on the previous page, the image captures the movement and joy of what dancing is for me. Try to let yourself get lost in the feeling of your photo to find your words.

# Unearthing Your Artistic Adventurer

In this chapter, the deeply personal experience of looking at the body through photographs and poetry has invited you to look past the physical to see what your internal self has to say. Now, we will uncover gems from these insights to use in our artwork. Creations made from this place will be deeply personal to you. However, that doesn't mean that this personal reflection must be obvious to the observer. How much you reveal is always up to you.

ARTWORK BY KELLY BARTON

Consider an artist whose work you consider "happy" or "not very dark." Perhaps some artists come to mind whose work at first glance might bring up descriptive words such as *adorable* and *sweet* and *childlike*. Then, think about what he or she might be conveying with the next layer of the piece and the next and so on. For example, a "childlike" piece might be about recapturing pieces of childhood that the artist might have missed out on because of the family in which he/she lived.

When you first glance at artist Kelly Barton's work, you might immediately be drawn to the happy colors she uses, the various collage pieces and fun, big shapes. If you aren't looking carefully, you might miss the many layers and darkness that can be found in some of Kelly's pieces.

I asked Kelly about this contrast in her work, and she explained that her work often represents the inner struggle a person has as she appears one way on the outside but feels another way when alone. We talked about how someone can seem happy and carefree at times, but no one really knows what another is struggling with in a given moment. This kind of internal contrast is part of what Kelly conveys in her work.

When creating this piece, Kelly began writing a poem using the prompt "My heart beats the story of _____." She explained that while writing, some darker images from her past made their way into the poem. When creating this mixed-media painting, she was drawn to sift through the lines of the poem until she found the one line she wanted to share: "Little girl blonde, blue." Even though the writing that came from this deeper place within her is not shared in its entirety in the piece, those layers are still part of this artwork just as they are part of the person who created it.

## The Excavator's Notebook:
### Body Observations

As you think about the poems and photographs you have created while focusing on your body, what observations have you uncovered? Remember that you do not have to share these observations with anyone else, so you can dive in and be as honest as you need to be while being gentle with yourself at the same time.

Let's look at another artist's work who also examines the body and mind's internal dialogue. Contributing artist Stephanie Lee thought about the prompt "I see me" and how this relates to the body when creating these two pieces. Looking at them is almost like looking at a page in an art journal as they are clearly from a deeply personal place. Even though the meaning that these pieces convey might not be clear, her use of photographs of herself invites us to know they have been created with a self-portrait in mind.

In both pieces she used watercolor paper, paint, self-portrait photographs, fabric, thread and other collage material. To help the photos blend into the pieces a bit more, she painted over them with acrylic paint. Within this process she uses all types of photographs (photocopies, ink-jet printed, laser printed) and first gently brushes clear gesso (she likes Liquitex) over them to prevent the ink from running when she paints.

Stephanie explained that the piece that includes her face is about the seeds of an idea growing and becoming. She has been pushing herself to see how these ideas have come into being and how she has been the catalyst for this. The second piece is about finding her footing as the ideas grow. Again, she is working with the image of pushing herself to actually see that the footing is there—a recognition of her own wisdom.

**ARTWORK BY STEPHANIE LEE**

84

## IN THE STUDIO:
# LET THE LAYER SPEAK FOR YOU

When you use layering techniques in your artwork, only you know what each layer represents. As you work with this exercise, notice the layers you add to your piece and the secrets these layers might be hiding from the viewer.

**TASK:** Let the layers of your mixed-media creation tell a personal story.

**NOTES:** Layers can take many forms. A particular color might represent a memory or an emotion. Maybe it's a layer you want to acknowledge and include but then wash over with a contrasting color. Perhaps you can write your story or thoughts of your story on strips of paper, and those can be layered between washes of color or other media. Words can be written as the beginning layer on a piece of watercolor paper or as a final layer on top of several layers of paint and paper. Consider using the poetry you wrote in this chapter as a creative prompt like Kelly did in her piece. Think about which layers of your story you want hidden or obscured and which ones you want to be seen clearly.

## IN THE STUDIO:
# FOCUS IN

Bring your self-portrait photographs into your studio and let yourself literally become part of your artwork.

**TASK:** Use a self-portrait photo as the focus of your creation.

**NOTES:** Consider using one of the self-portraits you have taken as part of the exercises in this chapter. Perhaps one of your "where you stand" photos can be the focal point for your piece. If you prefer to use another photo that isn't actually a self-portrait, but is of something that represents you, go for it. Think about the following possibilities:
• You can paint over a photo as Stephanie has done in her two pieces.
• A photo can be hand-stitched to a canvas or a piece of art on paper.
• Create a pocket on your artwork—the front or the back—so that your photo can be removed and examined more closely.
• Tear your photo into two or more pieces and then repair it directly on your artwork, using tape, gel medium or stitching.

# CHAPTER 5: *I look closer*

Frida Kahlo said, "I paint self-portraits because I am so often alone, because I am the person I know best." As you explore the topic of faces in this chapter, you will look at how really seeing yourself invites you to recognize this truth: You *are* the person you know best. Through this investigation of faces, you will also look beyond the physical and turn your attention inward.

Each day, we look at ourselves in mirrors many times, thousands of times in a lifetime. What are we looking at when we quickly glance at our reflection? Are we just checking to see that our hair is in place? Are we taking the time to really see ourselves?

In 2006, I read an article in *Yoga Journal* written by Elizabeth Gilbert. She talked about a teacher who had given her the practice of spending a few minutes a day looking at herself in the mirror. A few minutes might not seem like a lot of time, but when you are taking time to look yourself in the eyes and not hurry on to the next thing, it can seem like hours. Since reading the article, I have used this practice as a way to reconnect with myself during times when my inner dialogue was not so positive. Sometimes it will be my daily practice for several weeks. Other times I will simply take the time to look myself in the eye when I feel I most need to. For me, this exercise is an invitation to become more intimately connected with myself as I see beyond how I "look" and focus on who I truly am.

In this chapter, you will get comfortable looking closer as you take self-portraits of your reflection, shadow and face. You will examine how writing about your reflection reveals pieces of your internal dialogue, and then look at how you can push yourself even further as you combine photography and poetry. Also, you will explore creating faces to add to your artwork and examine different ways self-portraits can appear in mixed media.

Before we get started though, let's examine the mirror meditation. This meditation gently pushes you to spend time with yourself and your breath and to allow your inner thoughts to soften as you look yourself in the eyes.

# *Delving Into the Quiet:*

# MIRROR MEDITATION

As always, set aside a time when you won't be interrupted and can be in the quiet. You might have a mirror in your bedroom or bathroom that will work for this meditation. Perhaps you have a hand mirror you can prop up and use. After you decide where you will meditate, find a comfortable way to sit so that you can look into the mirror and see your face. Standing is also an option—I actually often do this meditation standing in the bathroom or looking in our hallway mirror.

This meditation can be done for a few seconds or several minutes. I invite you to spend at least thirty seconds the first few times and then work up to a few minutes. I usually spend about five to ten minutes with this meditation. When you first do this meditation, try the following:

Take a moment to find your center. Let your next inhalation begin there.

As you breathe, begin to reflect on the word acceptance. What comes to mind? An image? An idea? A feeling? When you are ready, bring your mind to the idea of self-acceptance.

With your next inhalation, begin to invite self-acceptance into your center. As you exhale, let this self-acceptance settle over you like a blanket.

After a few breaths, open your eyes and look in the mirror in front of you. Continue to breathe from your center, connecting with the self-acceptance that resides there, that is a part of you.

Notice where your mind travels. Breathe your way into the feelings. Try to let go of any judgment that arises. When you are ready, let the mind rest in the center of the body, in this place of self-acceptance.

**NOTES:** You can also work with the "Finding the Breath" meditation from the previous chapter (page 69) and simply look at your reflection and focus on your breathing. Another idea is to inhale compassion and exhale that compassion over you as you look eye to eye with yourself.

Also, try not looking away from your face during this exercise. If you feel overwhelmed, close your eyes for a breath or two. Then, open them and continue the meditation.

# Seeking Light and Shadow

As we begin to dive deeper into self-portraiture, we will explore taking photos of our reflections and faces. My hope is that through working with the Mirror Meditation (on the previous page) and taking time to look yourself in the eye, your self-portrait photo sessions will become a personal journey of discovering new ways to see yourself.

# PHOTOGRAPHY EXCURSION:
# REFLECTIONS AND SHADOWS

When I started taking self-portraits, I began to notice how my reflection and my shadow would appear in unlikely places. Do you already do this? Do you notice how your shadow follows you at different times of day? In this exercise, we find our shadows and our reflections, and we capture them.

**TASK:** Grab your camera and head out on a photo exploration to discover places your shadow and reflection appear.

**NOTES:** Time of day and location should be taken into consideration if you are setting out to find your shadow. Bright, harsh sunlight, often in the afternoon, can bring out the best shadows. When seeking reflections, look for mirrored surfaces (even the side of your toaster is an example), water and windows. Perhaps you will want to capture other people's shadows and reflections alongside your own.

**EXAMPLE:** These photos illustrate some of the reflection and shadow photos I took while on a few adventures with my husband during the summer of 2009 and on one chilly winter day.

PHOTO BY LIZ LAMOREUX

While visiting the Science and Industry Museum in Chicago, we were resting for a bit when a huge jet in one of the exhibits suddenly turned on its lights and created this opportunity for fantastic shadow photos on the blank wall behind us.

My journey with self-portrait photographs began after discovering a Web site called Self-Portrait Challenge (then called Self-Portrait Tuesday), started by Kathleen Ricketson, which is now a Flickr group. The site posted a monthly theme and then participants posted a response to the theme, through a self-portrait photograph, once a week on their blogs or on Flickr. This challenge pushed me to dig deeper into the feelings that came up when taking photos of myself. It also invited play and imagination into my photography (and daily life) as I brainstormed how to respond to the themes. In addition, the photo often inspired a written response, though sometimes my writing facilitated the idea for a photograph.

A window I discovered while on vacation in Michigan. When I took this photo, I had no idea Jon was taking a photo at the same time. Serendipitous surprises may arise as your family starts taking just as many photos as you do when they see you carrying your camera everywhere and get the bug themselves.

During a trip to the Oregon coast, Jon and I followed our shadows for a bit on the sand around us.

While on a winter walk near Puget Sound, I came across my reflection in a puddle.

Through this new awareness of enjoying self-portrait photography, I began to notice opportunities to take self-portraits while out in the world. As you take your camera with you, you will notice these opportunities too. It becomes an adventure to find yourself looking back at yourself in unexpected ways.

One of my favorite ways to capture a self-portrait is to use a mirror. In fact, you can find me taking self-portraits in the oddest of places when I discover a mirror (or mirrored surface). I have been known to be in the middle of a meal with a friend and suddenly grab my camera because I spot a mirror in the restaurant. I captured a self-portrait in the bathroom at the Ritz-Carlton in Chicago because the bathroom's ornate chandelier was reflected in the mirror and became part of the photograph.

I asked a few of this book's contributing artists to share some mirror self-portraits, such as the one you see of me, here. Each photo conveys a different mood, angle and aspect of the person's face or body.

This self-portrait was taken at my great-aunt's 90th birthday party. This mirror is in her son's home. I like the narrow view it gives as it shows just a piece of me and the world behind me.

On a day at Mount Rainier National Park, I suddenly saw my own very clear reflection in Jon's sunglasses and snapped away.

Stephanie Lee's self-portrait shows just a portion of her face, which sets a mood for this photo. The softness of the light and contemplative look seem to almost give us insight into her thoughts in this moment.

Susannah Conway has not only captured her reflection but also one of her beloved Polaroid cameras in this self-portrait.

Kelly Barton often takes self-portraits such as this one in this mirror in her home. I love how it includes the happy green walls behind her, giving us a bit more insight into her world.

## BEHIND THE LENS:
# MIRRORED FACES

Have fun exploring different settings and different light as you capture your reflection.

**TASK:** Take photos while looking in the mirror.

**NOTES:** Consider the various mirrors you have around your home and experiment with several of them. Take close photos and then some photos that capture more of your face and body. Remember, you can always crop them in a digital photo-processing program. Capture the edges of the mirror and your camera in the photo. As usual, this photo experience simply should be fun.

## Tools for the Journey:
## Cropping

Let the cropping function of your digital photo-processing program be your friend. I sometimes crop my photos to remove items I don't want (from unwanted body "things," such as an angle of my arm I do not like, to the laundry that always shows up in the background when I use the laundry room/bathroom mirror for self-portraits). It is also fun to play with the shape of your photo, for example, turning a rectangular photo into a square one.

Remember, if you aren't shooting raw files (and most of us who are not professional photographers are not), manipulating the photo does degrade it. This means if you crop quite a bit of the photo away, you might be left with a very small photo (which might be fine for sharing online but not printing). Try to shoot your photos on the highest resolution setting your camera allows, knowing that you might be cropping information out later.

**PHOTOS BY LIZ LAMOREUX**

Where I live, in the Pacific Northwest, winter is often filled with gray days that suddenly bring a few minutes of blue sky. When blue sky appears, I push myself to stop what I am doing and get outside for a few minutes. The following photos are from a midwinter day when I took my camera outside and captured myself in the peeking-out-for-a-bit sunshine. Note that I took all of these photos with my arms outstretched and did not use a timer or a tripod. As a result, I took a lot of photos on this day because an arm-outstretched-while-holding-the-camera technique is pretty hit or miss (sometimes I missed my face entirely). I also wanted to capture a wide range of emotions on my face, so sometimes I smiled, closed my eyes, relaxed my face and so on.

I asked contributing artist Jen Goff to take a series of face self-portraits that illustrate the idea of seeing more than just the face when looking at the photo. Her self-portraits often push away the surface feelings one might usually see in a photo and invite the viewer to go even deeper to notice the mood or theme of the photo. When I look at Jen's self-portraits, I often think about how they convey an essence of who she is.

I asked Jen about why she is drawn to self-portraits. She explained that she likes that she can control the energy that she puts into each photo. She wants her self-portraits to feel close and intimate, as though you are getting a glimpse into her private world. One aspect of Jen's self-portraits I have noticed is that she is seldom smiling. She explained that she thinks we're used to seeing smiling portraits and she wants to introduce other feelings into her images.

Even though Jen's photos seem to have a more "serious" tone, it's important to note that she deeply enjoys the experience of taking them. Because she is in control of the images, she experiences a freedom to express and unfold in front of the camera in a way that is more liberating than experiences where someone else is behind the lens. She encourages people who are approaching self-portrait photography for the first time to let go of how they feel about photos of themselves. When they do this, she believes they will feel the freedom that comes with being in control.

One interesting point that Jen's photos illustrate is that one can take incredible photos anywhere. If you look closely, you realize she is taking these photos while lying on the floor in her home. Through cropping and camera placement she captures all these moods. Jen says she crops out distractions that take away from the image because she wants the viewer to feel intimately connected to a piece of who she is.

PHOTOS BY JEN GOFF

## BEHIND THE LENS:
# CAPTURING YOUR ESSENCE

Give yourself permission to relax into this exercise. Try to capture your face from different angles as you seek a glimpse of the inner you.

**TASK:** Use your camera's timer to take photos of your face.

**NOTES:** Consider various locations in your home or backyard for this photo shoot. I often put my camera on a table and sit in front of it to capture my face. Sometimes I stand in front of a bookshelf or taller shelf in my home where the camera can rest. Taking photos with your arm outstretched holding the camera is also an option, but take several shots because this is often a hard angle to catch. When thinking of locations, consider a nearby park or nature preserve that is usually quiet so you can take these photos in solitude and in natural light.

# Revealing the Poet Within

We begin this section with a little reading to discover the poetry that speaks to us. If you are not familiar with many poets, never fear! Although academic poetry scholars have their own opinions about poetry, I believe that one of the most important aspects of poetry for the rest of us is that it is accessible. By this I mean that, as the reader, you feel that the poem is approachable, and although you might not understand each nuance, you are drawn to want to understand. We live in a time in which many poets are writing personal poetry, which tends to be more accessible and relatable. Let's take some time to find poetry that speaks to you.

## WORDS DISCOVERED:
# FIND A POEM FOR THIS DAY

Reading the words of others is a good way to jumpstart your own creative process.

**TASK:** Spend a little time with poetry. Find a poem that evokes an internal reaction. Write about this reaction.

**NOTES:** Take a trip to your favorite book-store and find the poetry section. Select a few books written by poets you are familiar with (or look at www.lizlamoreux.com/inner-excavation for suggestions), find a place to sit, and begin to read. Don't feel like you have to read the entire book, just read a few poems here and there. Stop when you find one that speaks to you. Feel free to move on to the next book if the first one isn't quite what you need. This has nothing to do with the poet but instead speaks to what you are drawn to in this moment. You are on a quest to find the poem you need to read today. If you already have a library of poetry in your home (or even just a couple of books), head to your bookshelf and spend time finding a poem that evokes a reaction. Also, consider looking at a few poetry Web sites to find a poem that speaks to you. I often find that a poem I merely liked in the past can hit me suddenly with words I needed to read on a certain day. This is the power of poetry. Find the poem that makes you gasp out loud or laugh or pause and take a deep breath. Keep looking. You will find the poem you need. When you do, write about your reaction to the poem.

Let's turn again to the mirror meditation you explored at the beginning of this chapter. If you've spent some time with this meditation, have you noticed your own internal dialogue? In this meditation, I have invited you to focus more on your breath rather than the mind chatter. However, if we decide to look at that mind chatter with intention—to let it be more like a whisper than of a cacophony of sea-birds—we can uncover some interesting pieces of who we are.

For example, I wrote the following poem after spending time looking at my reflection and the experience of meeting my own staring eyes.

## REFLECTION

*The hand sweeps mahogany hair across the forehead, then tucks strands behind the ear and adjusts the turquoise beaded earring. The fin-gertips trace the ruby rose mouth, pausing at the plump bottom lip as a thought prompts a tooth to catch the edge. The gaze, eyes to eyes, brown swirled caramel truth. The thought,* is this who I am, *rests inside the rhythm of each lowered lid.*

As we think about what this inner dialogue reveals to us, we can move past simply look-ing at our faces and turn toward the inward journey of looking closer at ourselves.

On the following page, Darlene Kreutzer turned her attention inward with her poem "sugar and petals." You will notice that the poem does share some physical descriptions, but the poem is really about looking under-neath to reveal pieces of where she has been and how looking beyond what was expected of her brought her to where she is now.

# SUGAR AND PETALS

Darlene Kreutzer

little girls and
sugar and spice
sweet smelling flowers
gold tinsel smiles

scuffed jeans and
skinned knees
a bruise on her elbow
a chip on her tooth

climbing as high
to the top of the bark covered
tree
to peer at the world
through the sunlight
green
not as transparent
as she wished
she could be

dirty sneakers
sweat trickled down
easier to pull the heads
off pretty barbie
then to face
insecurities
of the perception
of what it was to be
sugar and spice
and everything nice

puppy dog tails
and dirt under fingernails
seemed more interesting
and powerful
to a pigtailed fort builder

until one day,
she closed the book

on the fairy tale
realizing
sugar and spice
and pretty coloured petals
were a longing
in a heart
that thought carrying
a boy chip was easier
than being who
her heart longed
to be

so she sat down
on her gold plated
dream
wiped the icing from her fingers
and let the petals
flow from her smiles.

PHOTO BY DARLENE KREUTZER

As in Chapter 2, Darlene has paired a photograph with her poem. I asked her about why she is drawn to often pair the two. She explained that people sometimes say that she writes like she is painting with a paintbrush as she creates images with her words. She believes this is true, because she sees poetry as an image and often sees photography as a poetic act. Sometimes she uses the pairing of the two as a marriage and other times she wants them to contrast one another.

I asked Darlene if one tends to come before the other, and she explained that it depends. When she needs to work something through in her mind, she will often take long photography walks because taking photos helps her focus. Because she takes a photo while having an internal dialogue about something specific, that dialogue will resurface, even years later, when looking at the photo. This inner dialogue often becomes a writing prompt for the poem. Sometimes, when she is stuck creatively, she will pull out a photo from months or years ago and use it as a writing prompt. Other times, she will write a poem and look for the photo that captures the feelings the poem evokes in her. Again, she remembers this inner dialogue from the day she captured the photo.

## ON THE PAGE:
# A SELF REFLECTION

If you can, politely shut the door on your inner critic as you notice threads of thought in this exercise.

**TASK:** Write about, or to, your reflection.

**NOTES:** You may want to spend a few moments looking in the mirror or closing your eyes and picturing your own reflection. Try to let the racing thoughts quiet, and focus on your breathing. Invite your mind to focus on a single thread of your thoughts as you describe your reflection. Then go to the page (computer or paper) and simply write. Allow yourself to let go of any judgment of your words or of your reflection, and find your way to words and images.

## ON THE PAGE:
# INWARD INVESTIGATION

The pairing of a poem and a photo can uncover additional layers of meaning.

**Task:** Reveal another piece of the inner you by pairing a photo with an "I am" poem.

**NOTES:** In Chapter 1, we looked at writing a poem beginning with or prompted by the words "I am." You have probably noticed that the contributing artists have each written "I am" poems in the Artist Illuminations and have paired these poems with a photo. Thinking about all that you have examined so far in your *Inner Excavation* journey, write another "I am" poem and then pair it with a photo. You could also begin with a photo that prompts the poem. Note that the photo does not have to be a self-portrait. Looking at the Artist Illumination photos as examples, you can see that each person has a different interpretation of the answer to the question, "Who are you?"

# Unearthing Your Artistic Adventurer

At this point, you might have noticed a repeated invitation to see all that we create as a version of a self-portrait. Even if, at first glance, the artist does not appear literally in his or her piece, the very person who created it is, of course, present merely because it was made by his or her energy. When we consciously choose to bring ourselves into our artwork, we continue on the journey to uncover who we are in this moment and perhaps who we hope to be in the next.

Journals are intimate illustrations of where a person is on her path. Judy Wise created a mixed-media journal that examines faces while also looking at the symbolic idea of what a self-portrait can be. Judy decided to create a "transparent" journal because she believes that "in our journals, we become knowable to ourselves, things become 'clear' and 'transparent'" to us. Judy's words take me back to the Frida Kahlo quote introduced at the beginning of this chapter; think about the truth in her words that you are the person you know best. And how, through your artwork, you can continue to find yourself.

   By adding some of her personal art journal pages to this mixed-media journal, Judy has revealed pieces of herself in a more metaphorical self-portrait. She did not paint her own face (although faces are present), yet we know we are seeing her in this creation. Think about how our journals might be, for some of us, our most true and transparent self-portraits.

ARTWORK BY JUDY WISE

# ARTIST ILLUMINATION
## INTERVIEW WITH JUDY WISE

Here is glimpse into how Judy sees herself.

**Who are you?**
*I am above all curious. A lover of materials, of people, of observation and quiet. I want the answers to all the questions, and I want to investigate all the places, peoples and mores of the tribes. I am a seeker and a maker of things. I love life so much.*

**Who or what inspires you?**
Lao Tsu's *Tao Te Ching* from the translation by Gia-Fu Feng and Jane English. That book and several other reminders of what life is really about have gotten me through the darkest hours.

**How do you nurture yourself?**
I take as much time as I need to write in my journal each morning. Few things interrupt this pattern as it really clears my head and helps me plan my day. And if I want a treat, I have it. I listen to my body.

**How did you find your creative voice?**
My creative voice is still a mystery to me. I have no idea what it's all about. I just know that since I was a child I've been outgoing, from acting on the stage to dancing to singing and painting. I didn't say I did any of these things well, but I always did them with great gusto.

**JUDY'S RESPONSE TO "WHO ARE YOU?"**

## Tools for the Journey:
### Judy's Painted Face Tips

STUDY AND DRAW: Look at diagrams of the underlying bone structure, perspectives of eyes, noses, lips and ears.

FIND A NEW PERSPECTIVE: Walk your drawing over to a mirror and look at it as the mirror shows it.

TRACE: Use tissue paper to trace photographed faces to study the placement and sizes of the features relative to the head size.

PRACTICE: Remember that professional musicians practice 8–12 hours a day. If you are dedicated, you will learn very quickly how to create a face.

# IN THE STUDIO:
## PORTRAIT OF YOU

Before you begin this exercise, write down your own definition of a self-portrait. Then, brainstorm how this definition might influence what type of self-portrait you choose to create. You might want to tweak the definition as you form the idea for this self-portrait.

**TASK:** Create a mixed-media self-portrait (that might or might not include your face).
Consider the following ideas:

- Paint over a photograph like Stephanie Lee did in Chapter 4 (page 84).

- Emulate Norman Rockwell and grab a hand mirror and start sketching, painting your own face on the page/canvas.

- Let go of the need to draw/paint your face and instead add a photograph of yourself that you do not alter.

- Add words or pieces of the poems you wrote earlier in this chapter to your creation and let those words be your self-portrait.

- Don't worry about making a realistic face. Use Judy's face tips and just get started. Perhaps your face will have a cartoonish quality to it or maybe you even want to create a stick figure.

**NOTES:** Maybe you already feel comfortable painting faces; try creating a face with fabric or clay. Create a doll that looks like you. Maybe you took a workshop in mosaics but haven't revisited the technique; create a mosaic self-portrait or a self-portrait in any medium you want (paper, tile, fabric and so on). Think about all the other techniques you could use when creating a self-portrait.

# IN THE STUDIO:
## A JOURNAL OF FACES

The practice of creating faces, whether you are experienced creating them or just beginning, can become a daily creative meditation as you slow down and form these faces on the page.

**TASK:** Create a journal of faces. Consider the following ideas:

- Take your journal with you to cafés and begin to sketch the faces of the people you see.
- In the painting workshops I have taken, instructors have mentioned painting over the faces of women in catalogs and magazines to teach
  yourself about the shadows and contours of a face. Paste some magazine photos into your journal and start painting.

- Use tracing paper to capture the outline of a specific face from a magazine or photo and then use transfer paper (graphite paper) and retrace your image onto your journal page. Then fill in the details with your desired medium.

- Print out several photos of your own face, paste them into your journal and then paint over them.

- Think about other ways you might want to create faces in the mediums you enjoy working with.

**NOTES:** If you already know how to bind a book or want to learn how to do so, you might want to make your own journal. However, you could also start with a journal filled with thick, watercolor pages and simply begin. Review Judy's tips for creating faces. And remember, no one needs to see your work. Just play and have fun. If faces don't interest you, consider doing the above exercise focusing on a different part of the body, such as hands or feet.

# CHAPTER 6: *I open my heart*

Y ou are not on your journey inward alone. This is a simple but important truth to recognize and honor as you look at where you are on your path. In this chapter, you will look at how you open your heart to other people in your world and how you might want to invite some of these people to be a part of your creative travels.

During the last few years, I have found myself standing in the middle of an incredible community of women who are walking their paths, finding their way, working on claiming who they are and where they want to go. The connections I have made have been with people ready to show up and do the work that is such an important part of this life. We challenge each other; we listen to one another; and we hold the space for each other. However, my life hasn't always been filled with such intimate, strong bonds of friendship.

Throughout my life, I have had moments when I felt alone, not knowing if there was anyone out there who might "get" me and care about the thoughts, hopes, dreams that whirl around this brain and heart of mine. Then there have been moments when I thought someone or a group of friends saw me. However, then I found that I really wasn't feeling like my true self at all with these people, or when I did feel comfortable enough to share pieces of me, I was rejected.

After these experiences, I spent time digging in and working on *me*. I realized I had to figure out where I stood on my own path. Through these lessons, I have found that showing up as *me* is the best way to find the people who will see me.

You are a member of different communities as you travel in your life. Recognizing how members of these communities impact you is a necessary piece of your internal puzzle. I believe that the way to find your community is to do the heavy lifting of looking inward to see where you are and begin to understand where you want to go.

As you work through this chapter, you will explore ways to bring people into your creative wanderings to share the experience and learn from one another. You will examine collaborating through photography, including taking portraits of one another. You will look at ways to share poetry prompts, and finally, you will dive into the idea of collaborating on mixed-media projects. As you read and experience this chapter, think about other ways you can bring collaboration into your inward journey.

**Excavator's Notebook:** A Sense of Community

Think about the various communities in your life. How do you feel or not feel a part of these communities? When you think about inviting people into your creative world, who comes to mind? Do you already have creative companions, or are you seeking more kindred spirits?

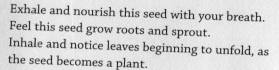

# Delving Into the Quiet:

# COMPASSION MEDITATION

Compassion meditations can be quite powerful as we bring images of those we care about into our quiet space. There are several compassion meditations out in the world, so the following is just one example. I find that giving my mind something to focus on can make the experience of the meditation a bit more tangible. After you practice this meditation several times, you will probably be able to tap into the compassion that rests around your heart a bit more easily. Then, you might be able to access the image of inhaling and exhaling compassion for yourself and others without needing an additional image. However, start with this and see where it leads you in your moments of quiet. As with the other meditations in this book, find a comfortable way to sit in a space where you will not be interrupted.

Settle into your body, letting go of your day with each exhalation.
Notice the subtleties of the way your body moves as you breathe.
Continue letting go with each exhalation.
Let your next inhalation begin at your heart center.
Feel your chest open and expand around your heart.
Exhale to create even more space.
Continuing with this awareness of your breathing and this space at your heart center. Imagine that inside your heart there is a seed; this seed represents compassion.
As you inhale, give this seed the space it needs to grow.

Exhale and nourish this seed with your breath.
Feel this seed grow roots and sprout.
Inhale and notice leaves beginning to unfold, as the seed becomes a plant.
Exhale and give this plant more nourishment.
Inhale and see the bud that forms on this plant inside your heart.
Exhale, letting go of anything that might prevent the growth of this plant.
Over the next few breath cycles, continue to breathe life into this plant and notice how this bud begins to unfold and bloom.
This flower represents the compassion that is blooming inside your heart.
Now imagine that this compassion is for you.
Breathe it in. As you exhale, let it wash over you.
Continue with this image for several breath cycles.
When you are ready, begin to imagine a person, animal or group of people who need this light full of compassion and love. Give yourself permission to work with whatever image you need to here. As you breathe, bring this person, animal or group of people into your heart.
With each inhale, the blooming, growing compassion within you surrounds them in compassion and love. With each exhale, anything not full of this compassion and love rolls off of you.
Continue breathing with your body's rhythm.
When you are ready, let go of the image you are holding in your heart and focus again on the blooming compassion that rests there.
Know that this space around your heart, the space that is ready to hold what you need, is within you always and is a source of compassion and love for you and for others.
Slowly bring your awareness back into your body, opening your eyes when you are ready.

# Seeking Light and Shadow

In the previous chapters, we have looked at using photography as a personal practice through the taking of self-portraits and through private photo adventures. This section introduces you to the process of inviting someone else into this personal practice, and how to share the experience of looking at the world through a camera lens. The experience can still be somewhat solitary as you each click your own camera, but you will open yourself to another's perspective as you collaborate.

# PHOTOGRAPHY EXCURSION:
# A SENSES COLLABORATION

In Chapter 2, we explored the senses as a tool in your creative toolbox. Let's look at the senses photography exercise again, but add the twist of collaborating with someone. This is another series I have on my blog (I call it "Senses: Views"), and I really enjoy that it is something that can be done with someone when you are together or experienced by two friends living on different sides of the country or world.

**TASK:** Ask a friend to take a photography senses journey with you. You will each take your cameras and photograph the senses at a particular location or look at the senses through a specific theme.

**NOTES:** When I ask a friend to join me on a senses collaboration, we usually choose a theme (especially because we are often not together when collaborating). This theme might be "a morning alone" or "reading and writing" or "the first day of spring." Choosing a theme gives us a place to start, but the theme is usually open-ended enough that we can each interpret it through our personal creative lens. If I am collaborating with someone in person, the theme might be "an afternoon together" or the name of the street, restaurant or park where we are spending time together. I explain that we are looking to capture the senses through the camera lens. Usually, I ask the person to choose his or her photos that represent the senses without talking to me. It is interesting to see what photos we choose without influencing one another. When presenting these photos, it is helpful to look at them as diptychs (meaning they are side by side) as the following
examples are presented.

**EXAMPLE:** Kristen Perman lives on the other side of the United States from me, and I always enjoy seeing the similarities and differences in the photos we capture as we both live near the ocean and bigger cities. We chose the theme of "water" for this series. Kristen sent me her photos from an afternoon at Coney Island, and I paired them with my photos of an afternoon along Puget Sound. In this case, we individually chose the sense associated with the photo before sharing them with each other.

*Hear*

PHOTO ON LEFT: KRISTEN PERMAN, PHOTO ON RIGHT: LIZ LAMOREUX

Know

See

Smell

Taste

Touch

PHOTOS ON LEFT: KRISTEN PERMAN, PHOTOS ON RIGHT: LIZ LAMOREUX

# ARTIST ILLUMINATION
## INTERVIEW WITH KRISTEN PERMAN

Here is a glimpse into how Kristen sees herself.

**Who are you?**

*I am learning and space, hidden inside leather and lace, creating as I blossom.*

**Who or what inspires you?**

The paintings of Mark Rothko and Robert Ryman. The photographer Cindy Sherman. Movie soundtracks such as *Bleu*, *Laurel Canyon* and *The Hours*. The writers John Irving and Mary Oliver. And even the sorrow and bittersweet poignancy of a movie like *Pan's Labyrinth* inspire me.

**How do you nurture yourself?**

With my husband's commuter train pass, I board the train heading east to Manhattan. In my pocket, music is loaded onto my iPod. My bag is packed with a novel and reading glasses, a small Moleskine journal and a couple of cameras, and I fall into the cadence of alone time.

KRISTEN'S RESPONSE TO "WHO ARE YOU?"

**How did you find your creative voice?**

When I left the design world, I was burned out. Other than reading fiction, I spent four years immersed in the world of science and medicine and separated myself from my creativity. In 2007, while working through *The Artist's Way*, I picked up a point-and-shoot camera to use for my artist dates, and my passion was ignited.

In Chapter 4, we began to give ourselves permission to experience the intimacy of turning the camera toward ourselves. In this chapter, we add another person to this experience but continue to focus on the joy and intimacy photography can bring us.

Vivienne McMaster and Darlene Kreutzer connected with one another in the world of blogging and became friends. Knowing they were both going to be at Squam Art Workshops in New Hampshire, I asked them to share their joy of taking portraits of others through a photo shoot together. Here is a glimpse into their experience.

After returning home and exchanging the results of their shoot, the two artists exchanged a series of letters, short snippets of which have been included here. To see the full version of the letters, you can go to www.lizlamoreux.com/inner-excavation.

**VIVIENNE'S PHOTO OF DARLENE**

**DARLENE'S PHOTO OF VIVIENNE**

**VIVIENNE'S PHOTO OF DARLENE**

*Dear Vivienne,*

*I loved photographing you, and it is my hope that someday there will be time for me to turn my camera on you again. These are my two favorite photographs of that afternoon. They are my favorite because this is how I see you, soft and wise and shining brightly, eyes that see more than most people and a voice that will gently share those feelings. I am also attaching the masked photograph because one of the most lovely parts of our photography session was something that I don't generally have with the clients I have shot in the past, is the adventurous artistic trust of just trying poses for nothing more than the joy of creating.*

*Do you know what I did when I saw your photographs of me? I stared in awe. You saw me. You really saw me. Also, you captured a stillness in me here that I am really trying to obtain in my life and which I get glimpses of when I meditate. This is the inner me that I am trying to become more often, and I love that you captured that instead of all the nervous frenzied energy that sometimes gets away from me. This has turned into such a powerful experience, photographing you, being photographed and reflecting on it all. The photo of me looking up at you, honestly, I think this is one of my favorite photos of me ever taken by someone and the more I look at it, the more I love it.*

*I learned so much from you. I learned that it is okay to let go of some the control I have, and that it was okay to feel awkward and unsure (and yes, even a bit shy), and that speaking about my insecurities didn't make them stronger but instead it made me let go of them a little bit.*

*Much love,*
*Darlene*

DARLENE'S PHOTO OF VIVIENNE

VIVIENNE'S PHOTO OF DARLENE

*Dear Darlene,*

*I, too, was nervous to have my picture taken, as I would have to relinquish that control and just trust you. You, who I have gotten to know through reading your words over these last few years. You, who takes such beautiful portraits and has a way of making people feel seen. You, who makes each person feel so special simply by the way you look them in the eye. I trusted you.*

*In one photo you captured what I find eludes me in almost all photos that are taken of me or that I have taken of myself. I was amazed that in one photo you would be able to show me such a precious part of my identity.*

*It's such a vulnerable thing to sit in front of someone and trust them to capture their vision of you with love. Often in photo sessions where I am the subject, I turn into a bad catalog model and get stiff and awkward. You pulled me out of that and gave me the guidance to capture the image you had in your mind.*

*I am so grateful that we got the chance to open up creatively to each other, to be vulnerable together as subjects and photographers. When we let ourselves be seen in all our awkwardness and vulnerable bits, we have so much more to offer each other. I'm so glad we could be that safe space for each other. I'm so grateful for it.*

*With so much heart,*
*Vivienne*

DARLENE'S PHOTO OF VIVIENNE

**Tools for the Journey:**
Darlene's Portrait Tips

I asked Darlene for a few tips about taking photos of others and how to find a good portrait photographer (because I highly recommend spending an afternoon with a photographer who can really see you).

## TIPS FOR TAKING PHOTOS OF OTHERS

LISTEN: Before beginning to take photos, talk to the other person about what he or she does not like about themselves in photos. Listen to what the person says. Just because you love someone's big, beautiful smile doesn't mean that she thinks her smile captures who she really is.

BE A DIRECTOR: Don't be afraid to pose people. Even have them do things that might feel silly. For example, what might feel like an odd, exaggerated pose might look fantastic in the photograph.

SHOOT FROM DIFFERENT ANGLES: Most people look better with the camera higher than them, especially if the person is curvy. However, skinnier people might be shot better from below or straight on. Try all of these angles with the person because each body is different. Take lots of photos.

COUNT TO THREE: People often squint when photos are taken in bright sun. However, it is nice to have the sun reflecting in their eyes in the photo. Have the person close his eyes, take a breath, count to three and on three open his eyes wide.

WATCH OUT FOR REFLECTIONS: If someone is wearing glasses or if you can see any reflective materials through your lens, be certain that your reflection is not in the shot.

## TIPS ON SEEKING A PORTRAIT PHOTOGRAPHER

RESEARCH WHAT YOU WANT: Envision what you want first and look for photographers whose work reflects your vision. For example, if you love soft colors in photos, don't hire someone whose photos are bright and bold. Even if you like the photos, that photographer will be at a disadvantage and cannot deliver what you are already envisioning.

SEE EXAMPLES AHEAD OF TIME: Make sure the photographer has an online portfolio you can look through. E-mail the photographer and ask if you can look at a full session of photos to get a feel for more than the "best shots" he or she shows online.

ARRANGE A PRE-MEETING: Never hire a portrait photographer without first meeting and having a conversation. If you don't feel comfortable and "click," it won't work, so always do an interview, and ask for references.

READ OVER THE CONTRACT: Always ask to see the contract before you decide to go forward with the photographer. If this person does not have a contract, be concerned about his or her experience.

## BEHIND THE LENS:
# CAPTURING THE LIGHT OF OTHERS

Sharing a photography session with another person is a bonding, yet vulnerable experience. Be patient and take your time, and, most of all, remember it's supposed to be fun.

**TASK:** Ask a friend or family member if you can take some photos of them. Consider also asking them to take photos of you.

**NOTES:** Before you begin your photography adventure with this other person, spend time thinking about who this person is and what he or she represents to you in your life. You might want to even journal about this. Think about why you are drawn to this person. Brainstorm about the light within them that you are drawn to and how you might want to capture this light through photos. Consider making a list of the photos you want to take. For example, maybe this person paints, and you could capture his hands while he is working, but you could also think about capturing his face in concentration while he is painting. Perhaps your friend is a gardener so you want to capture her in her backyard amidst her flowers. Then push yourself to think even deeper about how she might also be the friend who her heart on her sleeve, so you might want to photograph her hands open to the world ready to love. Also, think about props you might want to bring to this photo shoot.

# Revealing the Poet Within

Writing is often thought of as a solitary exercise, but in this section, we explore a few ways to collaborate with others using the written word. Hopefully, this section will be a springboard for you to create your own collaborative writing exercises and experiences with the people in your life.

# WORDS DISCOVERED:
# GATHER AND SHARE

In this next writing exercise, you revisit the "Creating a Word Toolbox" exercise you looked at in Chapter 1 (page 19). This time, you will work with a friend and share the words you have discovered as prompts for a collaborative poetry exercise.

**TASK:** Pull out a book from your bookshelf, gather a list of words, and trade that list with a friend who has done the same. Then, write a poem inspired by and using some words from this traded list.

**NOTES:** You might use only one word from the list your friend gives you; just experience the thoughts and phrases that were shared.

**EXAMPLE:** Contributor Stephanie Lee and I traded word lists and then each wrote a poem inspired by the list. The word lists are included here because you might find a few words you want to use as prompts for your own poem.

The word list I sent Stephanie:

| | | | |
|---|---|---|---|
| delicate | wander | heartbeat | ash |
| presence | golden | sojourn | sun-flecked |
| labor | flux | mystic | crumb |
| twig | scatter | blaze | peony |
| petal | speckle | exchange | lavish |
| ample | farewell | recover | narrow |
| slope | whole | earthquake | cushion |
| violet | plunge | vine | creak |
| hum | voyage | sacrament | transparent |
| shimmer | grace | vision | extravagance |

The word list Stephanie sent me:

| | | | |
|---|---|---|---|
| vein | anxious | swag | true |
| leaning/lean | write | crisp | river |
| sage | regret | postcard | virago |
| highway | dialogue | seven | time |
| goldbeater | madness | arch | fish |
| crimson | silver | stone | Arthur |
| sprawling/ sprawl | delay | mist | native |
| moss | time | habit | linger |
| corner | wind | smoky | |
| church | bible | Tuesday | |
| | entry | edge | |

## STEPHANIE'S POEM:

A heartbeat at the end of a broken twig
where ash and grace and sun-flecked rain
are kneaded for a compress on the wound
Vision in flux, the sky blankets in wait
Until a fist of petals hums through the splitting salve
Opening.
An ample, earthquake soul takes its first breath.

## MY POEM:

Unclenching fear, I find
sprawling moss-covered twisting fallen trees
and crimson crooning grosbeaks
Arching my body to look closer, I see
wind twirling pages of regret
and smoky highways littered with habits
Inhaling deeply, I know
crisp, birthing-Spring Tuesdays
and the hope of lingering time

# ARTIST ILLUMINATION
## INTERVIEW WITH STEPHANIE LEE

Here is a glimpse into how Stephanie sees herself

**Who are you?**

*I am that moment just before sunrise when the
world is still chilled and warmth is whispering in.
I am the in breath before a belly laugh
The out breath after a hole is dug for a new tree
When the scent of the fresh earth draws in
through your skin.
I am the bark on the trunk,
The protective and durable husk that guards the tender
heart.
I am the heaving earth and the laughing roots.
I am the leaf on the tree, there—up from the tip of the
branch
Quivering with my brothers and sisters, leaning
To make room for the opulent bloom.
I am the curious bee that hovers near
Drawn close by the lure of the sweet scent,
I am the white on that bloom and the pulse in its stem
And the fragrance within that reminds you of being
reborn.*

**Who or what inspires you?**

The authors Julia Cameron, Natalie Goldberg, Annie
Dillard, Susan Wooldridge—just to name a few.
There are so many blogs written by people who are
shining such a bright and inspiring light into this
world daily. I am so deeply grateful for the highway
of information and inspiration that pulses so val-
iantly on through the Internet. I can't even begin to
start naming names.

STEPHANIE'S RESPONSE TO "WHO ARE YOU?"

**How do you nurture yourself?**

I write. I write in my journal to reacquaint myself
with the wisdom and trust that is inherent in my
spirit. I also find a centering and nurturing when I
spend time in observance of and interacting with
nature, specifically in growing plants of all kinds on
my property (and in my home).

**How did you find your creative voice?**

I can't really credit one thing for helping me find
my creative voice, but certainly keeping a journal
has been near or at the top of the list. In finding my
true spirit voice, I see the rising creative voice, and I
am learning to trust the vibration of it in my ears. It
is feeling more and more at home here, and I so look
forward to hearing how it grows and evolves for the
rest of my life.

Inviting someone into your creative space, literally and figuratively, can be a great way to spend an afternoon. At the same time, I see it as a brave act, especially when you invite them to join you in your writing world. To let people into the lines you write that share pieces of your innermost self is to trust them with part of who you are. This brave trust is a gift you give your friend. I believe that sharing our words, our poems, is a way to let someone else know, "This is me. This is who I am on my path." And then, when you ask that person to share something in return, you are given the gift of seeing your friend in a deeper way.

Photographs can be another prompt to help you find your way to a poem. Exchanging photos with another person can be a great prompt, especially when the photos are unexpected or something that you would probably not typically capture with your lens.

Contributor Jen Goff and I exchanged photos via E-mail and then wrote poetry inspired by the other person's photo.

**"SAND AND SHADOW" PHOTO BY LIZ LAMOREUX**

**"LONGING" PHOTO BY JEN GOFF**

Jen's poem in response to my "Sand and Shadow" photo:

*does the grain of sand hold:*
*tiny remembrances?*
*small echos of wishes unspoken?*
*recognition of truths?*
*longings?*
*collections of fallen wishes and lost songs?*

My poetry response to Jen's "Longing" photo:

*The sun streams her way*
*through the open window,*
*fresh possibility.*
*I am leaning in*
*toward all that might be*
*as I walk forward*
*into the gift*
*that is this day.*

117

The writing prompts throughout this book could all be used in a collaborative poetry or writing adventure. You could exchange word lists like Stephanie and I did in the "Words Discovered" exercise in this chapter. You might want to come up with "I statement" prompts to exchange with a friend. Perhaps you and your friend can exchange favorite poems and then each write a poem in response to the exchanged poem.

Kristen Perman and I blended the idea of a visual prompt and an exchanging poetry prompt in an exercise that we think of as a visual and written conversation in poetry. We started with a specific prompt, the title of this chapter, "I open my heart." I wrote a poem response to this prompt and passed it to Kristen. She continued the conversation through a photograph. I responded with a photograph, and then Kristen finished the conversation with a poem. One of my favorite aspects of this first conversation is that when I suggested to Kristen that I wanted to add another collaborative project to this chapter that involved a process of writing poetry back and forth using words and photos, she immediately said, "Oh, it can't be with me. I can't write a poem!" Yet, she did. I love poetry and the gifts it brings.

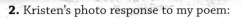

**2.** Kristen's photo response to my poem:

**1.** My poem using the prompt, "I open my heart."

*With soft, determined eyes and outstretched palms,*
*I turn toward all that rests before me*
*I open my heart*
*I sit in the stillness*
*And listen.*

**3.** My photo response to Kristen's photo:

**4.** Kristen's poetry response to my photo, which concludes this poetry conversation:

*The cold, gray, wintery sky*
*displayed before me,*
*shimmers with incandescence.*

## ON THE PAGE:
# POSTCARD POETRY

The image of pen pals sending postcards takes on a whole new meaning when you swap photos that become prompts for a poetry exchange.

**TASK:** Swap photos with a friend and use the photos as a prompt for a poem.

**NOTES:** Imagine the photo is the front of a postcard you are sending; let your writing be the back of this postcard. Maybe you will be inspired by one small aspect of the photo or the feeling the photo invokes. Push yourself to see the photo as a starting point for a poem. Don't feel like you have to connect your writing to the photo in an obvious way. Think about doing a series of poetry collaborations like this—one pairing your friend's photography and your words and vice versa. You could even send them to one another like postcards. Of course, you can also do this with your own photography as yet another prompt to add to your writer's toolbox.

## ON THE PAGE:
# A POETRY CONVERSATION

As you invite a friend into your world of poetry with this exercise, you will learn more about one another though this intimate conversation of poems and photographs.

**TASK:** Invite a friend to have a conversation through visual and written poetry.

**NOTES:** Consider following the same pattern Kristen and I did: Begin with a poem that you exchange with a friend, who responds with a photo, then you respond with a photo, then your friend responds with a poem. Maybe you will want to come up with your own pattern, but it is fun to make sure that each of you shares at least one photo and one poem in this conversation. This type of correspondence is one you could have through the mail, through E-mail or through your blogs. Have fun finding the poetry inside photography and the written word.

# UNEARTHING YOUR ARTISTIC ADVENTURER

Creating alongside another person not only brings in companionship during the creative process but also invites new perspectives, ideas and so many other things. Having attended several art retreats, I know the joy of sitting at a table with people and sharing supplies, chatting about life and experiencing synergy when you paint, stitch or twist wire together.

After attending several workshops, I found that I prefer creating with other people even though I don't get to do this as often as I would like. The creative energy of a group (whether it is two people or twenty) gives me an energy and a focus that I sometimes miss in my little room in my house.

I am lucky enough to have a few friends I spend weekends with every now and then. We bring out the paints or jewelry supplies to the kitchen table and have fun while we create something new as we chat and work side by side. One such friend is Kelly Rae Roberts. In Chapter 2, I introduced you to a painting I created while spending an afternoon with Kelly surrounded by paints and paper and ephemera (see page 43). Because she feels more comfortable with paint as a medium than I do, I deeply appreciated that Kelly brought her teacher-self along and gently gave me a few suggestions when I was stuck or doubted my intuition about what to do next. Whenever I look at the painting I completed when we were together, I remember the joy of that day and am so appreciative of our friendship.

Maybe you already have some friends you create with on a regular basis through a knitting group, art group or quilting bee. Maybe you want to create a group in your town or you have a friend or two who often say things like, "I wish I could paint/draw/sew like you." Inviting these friends over to play while you share a few of the things that you know is a wonderful way to get a group started. It might seem simple, but the exchange of information is a great way to break the ice with someone new or connect further with an old friend.

The people I have met through art retreats and through my blog—people who started out as "online friends" who have become deep, real, true friends—are my creative circle. They are the people I turn to when I am stuck or need support or just want to brainstorm the new crazy idea brewing inside of me. The truth is that they live all around the world, so getting together to create for a day or weekend just doesn't happen as often as I would like. Perhaps you experience this as well. Maybe your closest creative friends are a phone call/E-mail away instead of a short drive.

To ease this distance of miles between us, my friends and I work on creative projects together. These might be projects similar to the poetry and photography collaborations you have seen earlier in this chapter (because as simple as it is, collaborations that can be done through E-mail/blogging are easier than ones done through the mail). We also organize swaps (of craft/mixed-media supplies), work on collaborative creations and other fun things.

## The Excavator's Notebook:
### Creative Environment

Think about how you believe you "best" create. Do you prefer solitude? Why or why not? Have you invited a friend over to your studio space to play and create? Do you have creative friends you exchange ideas with in person or online?

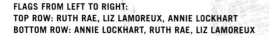

**FLAGS FROM LEFT TO RIGHT:**
**TOP ROW: RUTH RAE, LIZ LAMOREUX, ANNIE LOCKHART**
**BOTTOM ROW: ANNIE LOCKHART, RUTH RAE, LIZ LAMOREUX**

Contributors Ruth Rae and Annie Lockhart joined me in one such collaboration for this chapter. One fabric creation I enjoy making are prayer flags inspired by Tibetan Buddhist prayer flags. I asked Ruth and Annie to each create two flags (I gave them specific dimensions and asked them to start with a linen-colored piece of fabric) that were prompted by the phrase "I open my heart." I explained that I would create two as well and then sew all six flags together to form one set of flags.

We each focused on this prompt in different ways, and each flag truly represents the artist's style and what she is drawn to create with. Ruth's flags are in her signature colors of linen with machine-embroidered phrases inspired by the prompt. Annie's flags are full of vintage fabrics and other bits, and she gives the viewer permission to interpret the message these flags share through these colors and stitches. My flags combine paper and fabric and include a poem typed onto a pocket that will hold wishes and blessings for the person who will hang these flags.

# IN THE STUDIO:
# SHARING CREATIVE SPACE

If you are accustomed to working alone, break out of your normal routine and see where creating alongside of others might lead you.

**TASK:** Plan a studio day with a friend (or friends) and create side by side.

**NOTES:** This exercise is more about the community aspect of creating in the company of others and the joy and creative pushes that can come from that experience. A few ideas for your gathering:

- Ask your friends to bring paints and paper and collage together.

- Think about exchanging techniques with one another from week to week and have mini-workshops. Maybe one person enjoys creating jewelry and can share some wire-wrapping techniques, and the next week, a person who focuses on still-life drawing can instruct the group.

- Ask people to bring whatever creative project they are currently working on and just enjoy the company of one another as you work on your independent projects.

# IN THE STUDIO:
# COLLABORATE

Collaborating on artwork can connect you with other artists both locally and across the miles. Before you invite a friend or two to work with you on a project, think about the kind of community you want to create with this collaboration.

**TASK:** Ask a friend (or two or three) to collaborate on a piece of art. You might create in person, but you might also want to create with friends who live far away. Many collaborations can be done through the mail or a combination of mail and E-mail.

**NOTES:** Here are a few ideas to get you thinking about what you might collaborate on:

- Create a painting together. You might want to talk about an overall vision for your painting. You might want to pass it back and forth, each of you adding something new each time.

- Brainstorm something with several pieces, such as the prayer flag example in this chapter, and ask people to contribute.

- Create a journal of collage and poetry, using a chosen theme.

# CHAPTER 7: *I know*

When I first started thinking about what I wanted to share in this chapter, I kept hearing Barbara Streisand singing the chorus of "Putting It Together" from *Sunday in the Park with George*. The lines that kept repeating in my head were, "Bit by bit, putting it together. Piece by piece, only way to make a work of art. Every moment makes a contribution. Every little detail plays a part." The idea of putting each little piece together that you have looked at in the previous chapters and then combining them to make a work of art is what this chapter is all about.

During my two-year yoga teacher training, each student had to choose a topic to present as part of a final project. I chose the topic of journal writing as a spiritual practice. Because I was also finding my way in my creative community and was uncovering how important my own journal writing was to me, I looked at several different types of journaling, from writing to blogging to art journaling.

As I was researching this topic, I read several books and began to piece together a theme. When we are on a quest to find answers to the questions of our life, writing (and creating) is a way to capture the thoughts that emerge and teach us as we seek. This is what blogging and painting and poetry writing and photography have become for me: A way to gather notes of what I am learning in a way that pushes me to pay more attention. A journal (in whatever form it takes) can act as a portfolio for our *Inner Excavation* adventures.

This chapter focuses on various types of journals as a way to showcase the writing and photography we have explored in this book. We will look at everything from fabric journals to blogs as ways to illustrate our journey inward and remind us of where we have been and push us to envision where we want to go. In doing this, you can continue to notice what this journey is teaching you. My hope is that what you have learned will invite you to own all the truths you know.

# A SELF-PORTRAIT COLLAGE JOURNAL

Contributor Vivienne McMaster created this book in a workshop given by Marisa Haedike and Christine Mason Miller. The students in the class were instructed to think about a theme for their book and to bring photos and collage materials inspired by this theme. Vivienne, who lives in Vancouver, British Columbia, spent the summer in California and wanted to capture this adventure in a book. She took many solitary photo walks—where she often captured self-portraits—while on her trip and printed some of these photographs to take to the workshop.

Vivienne explained that when she started adding photos to her book, she began to realize how, when put together in this format, her photographs became a vessel to illustrate what she was sifting through and discovering internally during this time in her life.

## PUTTING IT TOGETHER:
# PHOTOS IN HAND

JOURNAL BY VIVIENNE MCMASTER

In this time of blogs and other online social networking sites where we share our photos, we sometimes forget the simple joys of printing out photos and displaying them in an accessible and a beautiful way.

**TASK:** Print out your digital photos and put them into a journal where you can look through them.

**NOTES:** Consider the following:

• Head to your local stationery story (or peruse a favorite online shop) and look for a journal or photo album to display your photos.

• Make a collage journal like Vivienne did using papers and other elements as visual backdrops for your photos. You can buy a premade journal or create your own book. There are several great journal making tutorials online that you can find with a quick Internet search.

• Maybe you currently spend time scrapbooking your family's adventures. Consider using some of the techniques you already know to make a scrapbook that is just about you.

# A STITCHED POETRY JOURNAL

The prompts in Chapters 2 and 3 of this book were the foundation for a fabric journal I created to house some of my poems inspired by my grandparents. The journal cover is created from some of my favorite items in my studio, and the vibrant colors made me very happy as I stitched them together. This vibrancy could seem like a contrast to some of the writing housed in the journal--a bit melancholy as I often use poetry to sift through my feelings and grief since the death of my grandparents. Yet, my grandparents have taught me many things, including how to really enjoy the experiences of my life, and this journal also reflects these truths.

I often use my vintage typewriter to get my poems onto a page (and out of my computer or random notebooks) so I can see them and hold them and let the words I have written sink into me. The act of methodically pushing each key of the typewriter and then using my sewing machine to stitch the poems to the pages of this journal has been an exercise in giving myself permission to learn from my own words.

## PUTTING IT TOGETHER:
# GATHER YOUR POEMS

Wherever you write poetry—on your computer, in a notebook and so on—it is always a good idea to put it someplace where you can easily find it, revisit it and share it with others (if you choose). A book is a perfect spot to showcase your words.

**TASK:** Gather your poems and poem notes together and put them in a journal/book.

**NOTES:** The point of this exercise is to get some of your poems into one place where you can look through them and soak up what you have written (and perhaps share your words with others). Ideas to get you started:

• If you enjoy sewing (or even if you just know how to use a sewing machine), consider gathering fabric, paper and other collage elements and making a fabric journal cover. (Visit www.lizlamoreux.com/inner-excavation, for more information about how to make a journal similar to the one I created for this project.) You could then either house another journal inside this cover or sew in pages.

• Type your poems into a word-processing document. Print them out and have them bound into a book (or bind them yourself).

• Gather up some favorite writing pens/markers and a blank book/journal, and spend some time writing your poems out one word at a time.

• Make or purchase a special box where you can store loose pieces of individual poetry.

JOURNAL BY LIZ LAMOREUX

129

# MIXED-MEDIA PHOTOGRAPHY JOURNAL

Contributor Jen Goff has created a deeply personal mixed-media journal that houses a few of her self-portrait photographs and snippets of her personal poetry. Jen uses several different photography mediums in this journal. She sometimes uses her Diana camera (a Diana is a plastic camera that takes 120-film) and a Polaroid camera when taking photos. She also likes to create photo transfers with her film camera and slide film. Because of Jen's use of film and how she manipulates her digital photos, the photographs in this journal take on an aged, almost vintage look.

When Jen created the photographs for this journal, she put a lot of intention in wanting to show emotion in her face and eyes. She wanted to invite the viewer to think about what she might be feeling and contemplating at those moments. When she takes self-portrait photographs, she hopes people will reflect on the layers that are not always obvious at first glance.

Jen shared that this journal represents how she was feeling in a deeply emotional time in her life. As a result, it gives the viewer insight--through photography and words--into this intense period of time. Yet, viewers might also see the emotion expressed in this book as a mirror to look inward at their own questions.

# PUTTING IT TOGETHER:
# TAKE ANOTHER LOOK

In this age of point-and-shoot digital photography, we can forget to explore the variety of photography tools out there. In the past two years, I have begun to use my film cameras again, which has pushed me to think a bit before snapping a photo. I don't have the luxury of taking ten or even twenty-five photos of the cherry tree blooming in my yard to find the "best one," and instead take just two or three from various angles after spending time thinking about how I want to capture the compositions. Using film becomes a more meditative exercise for me as I slow down in this way.

**TASK:** Revisit one of the photography prompts in the previous chapters of this book (or use one of these prompts as a springboard for your own idea), but this time use a photography medium that is new to you.

**NOTES:** Explore one of the following ideas:

• Take your old film camera for a spin.

• Convert your digital photos to black and white.

• Use a digital photo-processing program to apply textures and other effects to your photos.

• Invest in an instant camera (such as an Instax or Polaroid) or a toy camera (such as a Holga or Diana).

• Take photos with your phone (especially if you don't usually take photos with it).

• Use a new lens (perhaps you have recently purchased a macro or wide-angle lens or maybe you have a fish-eye or other lens you haven't played with yet).

**JOURNAL BY JEN GOFF**

# BLOGGING IT ALL TOGETHER

Artist Susan Tuttle's blog is a favorite of mine because she shares snippets of her experiences through various mediums, including her own poetry, photography and digital mixed-media art. This makes her blog visually appealing but also gives the reader an intimate slice of her world through her written word. Susan's blog is, to me, a true self-portrait of her life because she shares these glimpses of where she is, what she sees, where she has been. As the reader of her blog, you are invited to recognize her journey, and at the same time, you are pushed to turn inward yourself.

I asked Susan to share two "blog-like" journal entries that combine photography, her writing and her digital mixed-media artwork. The first includes three digital mixed-media pieces along with journal-like writing. The second features several photographs and a poem.

friends
poetry vacation
**art** snow

ART

IS ME UP

it is a simple morning
my heart feels big and warm.
there is snow
crackling fire
in the
woodstove
nowhere
to
go
today
accept
to follow
my heart.

*I feel beautiful when . . .*

*. . . I can experience the power of creating something—whether it be through my art, music, writing, cooking, homemaking, whatever it may be. Creating art, taking photographs and writing are the modes of creativity that I am most drawn to, and consequently, they are the most powerful for me. They are like portals that transport and allow me to transcend beyond my human limitations. Creativity requires going inward to the depths of heart and generates a swirling of energy and powerful connection to something beyond ourselves—something I can't verbally name, but recognize with all that I am. The ego falls away as I go deeper into my work. Creativity comes* through *me, as opposed to* from *me. Fully engaging in the creative process is like meditation—it allows me to be present in the moment, quiets the chatter in my brain and infuses me with a feeling of purpose. Having outlets for creative experience promotes vitality and fills me with joy. If I go too long without it, it feels like a part of me is missing. I must create. It's not just a passion, but a necessity for the well-being and growth of my soul.*

*Each creation is an adventure. The fewer preconceived notions I have, the wilder the journey! Follow your internal compass— gravitate to what moves you; follow it, let the process unfold the way it was meant to. "Mistakes" can lead to serendipitous results that were meant to be—making the piece just right. Struggle is good. Wanting to throw your work in the trash is even better—then you know that things are just getting good.*

## LIFE CIRCLE

*Sunday morning*
*early October*
*hints of frost melting into dewdrops*
*i make my last visit to the garden*
*full of zinnias*
*before my mother-in-law puts them to bed for wintertime*

*brown, brittle, rattling bones in the chilly wind.*
*and to my surprise there are tender buds just beginning,*
*and ones in their perfect prime*

*i sit in the field*
*fixated on a decaying zinnia,*
*succumbing so gracefully to its natural death.*

*a church bell begins to ring in the distance*
*my eyes fill*
*my heart pulls tight*
*and i remain still*
*in the perfect beauty*
*of the moment*

*i am reminded of births*
*marriages*
*funerals*
*the people i love.*
*and i am comforted by the garden,*
*whispering to me*
*everything is just as it should be*
*as it was meant to be*

*i stay as long as i need to,*
*then rise and go*
*in peace.*

**DIGITAL ARTWORK BY SUSAN TUTTLE**

PUTTING IT TOGETHER:
# CREATE A PORTFOLIO OF YOU

Susan's blog posts illustrate ways to bring your poetry, photography and artwork together into an intimate visual portfolio. After experiencing all the prompts, exercises and visual examples in this book, think about how you are drawn to combine your writing, photography and artwork in your own visual portfolio that you can share with others.

**TASK:** Choose a few items from your *Inner Excavation* portfolio, and choose a format to share them with a few trusted friends.

**NOTES:** This is your opportunity to invite others into the world you have experienced as you have turned inward to do the heavy lifting throughout this book. Perhaps you already have a blog where you might consider sharing a poem or your self-portraits. Consider creating a book through an online self-publishing program to showcase your favorite personal pieces.

# ARTIST ILLUMINATION
## INTERVIEW WITH SUSAN TUTTLE

Here is a glimpe into how Susan sees herself.

**Who are you?**
*i am hungry . . .*
*. . . for less material things*
*. . . for more things that really matter—those*
*things that I can take with me when I leave my*
*earthly body*

**Who or what inspires you?**
The song "All About Soul" by Billy Joel, the
book *Writing Down the Bones* by Natalie
Goldberg and the poetry of Howard Nemerov.

**How do you nurture yourself?**
with:
art
music
writing
reading
photography
delicious food and drink
sleeping
connection
space
love
love
and more love
and I forgot to mention coffee

**How did you find your creative voice?**
It is a process that is mainly about deep
listening and following my heart. At times
I feel like I've found it, only to move on,
look back and realize I didn't find its full
potential yet.

SUSAN'S RESPONSE TO "WHO ARE YOU?"

137

# PARTING THOUGHTS

Now that you find yourself at the end of this book, I hope you have begun to feel comfortable owning the poet's voice that lives inside you. Perhaps you will now find yourself carrying your camera with you to capture the everyday and to find opportunities to take self-portraits. And, as you find yourself in your studio space, hopefully you are energized by the idea of adding inspiration from your poetry and photography to what you create.

We decided not to add a Resources page to the back of this book because many Internet resources often change and the number of books I wanted to list as inspiration was simply too long to include. However, I have created a Resources section on my Web site that will continually be updated. You can find it by visiting:
www.lizlamoreux.com/inner-excavation.

At this site, you will also find additional prompts, more information about the contributors and other tools to add to your creative toolbox that you carry with you on your journey.

I hope that you will continue to explore the themes presented in *Inner Excavation*. Maybe you will come up with your own prompts and invite others to join you on your adventures. My belief is that you can return to the prompts in this book repeatedly because each time you find the senses of a moment or capture your own reflection or create while directly inspired by your experiences, you dive further into understanding where you are on your path.

As you walk forward in your life, may your inward journey be full of illumination, possibility and moments to sit in the quiet to soak it all in.

# THE ARTISTS

**Kelly Barton** is a mixed-media artist and graphic designer. Most days, you will find her in her studio with music playing and colors flying. She is inspired by the workings of a girl's nutty mind and believes that growing up as a girl is really enough inspiration for any female artist. Her art has been part of several national shows, including: "Vision of Squam," "Core: The Art and Design of the Torso" and "The Enormous Tiny Art Show." Her work has also appeared in national publications, including *Underwired* (March 2008, cover). To put it simply: She is one happy girl, especially when she is creating in her studio.
Visit Kelly at www.campindigo.blogspot.com.

**Jen Goff** lives in Portland, Oregon and works out of her tiny studio. If you were to step inside you would find lichen, dried flowers, feathers, seedpods, jeweler's tools and a woman lost in creation. Visit Jen at www.paperwingspdx.com.

**Susannah Conway** is a photographer, writer and the creator of the Unravelling E-courses. She holds an HND in photography and a first-class degree in journalism, and spent many years working as a fashion editor and freelance journalist. After the death of her partner in 2005, Susannah was forced to reassess her path and found herself drawn back to photography. After setting up her own photography business in 2007, she began teaching local self-awareness workshops that used the camera as a tool for healing. Her photography and writing have been featured in many international publications, including *The Photo Album*, *Artful Blogging*, *Cosmopolitan* (UK) and *The Guardian* (UK). She lives in London, England, and is currently writing her first book.
Visit Susannah at www.susannahconway.com.

**Darlene J. Kreutzer** is a published photographer and poet who lives with her musician husband and sports-minded son in the city of Edmonton, Alberta—a province of prairie, rocky mountains, desert and forest in western Canada. When she is not scribbling in her notebooks or playing with light, she can be found sketching, playing with paints, twisting up jewelry designs or puttering in her kitchen and garden. While she has both an English Literature degree and a Secondary Education degree, she continues to take art and photography classes, hoping that she will continue to learn, grow and change as the years go by. She is grateful for all of life's possibilities.
Visit Darlene at www.hippyurbangirl.com.

**Stephanie Lee** is a seeker and a finder, an asker and a listener, a poet and a mute. She works with metal, plaster and paint, and she shares what she's learned with others through teaching. She lives for the biggest little things, like rainstorms and a house full of laughter and the sound of trumpets. She loves learning, sewing, cooking, making things for friends, generally being domestic, reading and writing and writing about what she's reading. She eats peaches over the sink and her insides like to boogie while outside she keeps a cool front. She loves green shoes and wearing them while perhaps driving a little too fast because she likes the way her stomach tickles when she goes over that little hill.
Visit Stephanie at www.stephanielee.typepad.com.

**Annie Lockhart** is a mixed-media assemblage artist, photographer, collector, designer and author. Annie teaches creative workshops with a focus on making heart-and-soul connections through the use of symbolism, memories and metaphors. Her artwork has been featured in national art magazines and can be found in juried fine art shows throughout the country.
Visit Annie at www.annielockhart.typepad.com.

**Vivienne McMaster** is a fine art and portrait photographer with a great love for toy and vintage cameras, self-portraiture and channeling joy through her camera and into an image.
Visit Vivienne at www.viviennemcmaster.com.

**Kristen Perman** lives in a suburban village close to NYC with her husband and daughter, working part-time as an acupuncturist and herbalist. In a previous life, she worked as a commercial interior designer, before leaving the art world for grad school and Chinese medicine. Combining a love of art and science, Kristen spends her time pursuing her passion behind the lens. She can be found roaming the corridors of Manhattan and the shores of New York and New Jersey in search of light and sea glass, as well as fire escapes and the shelves of second-hand bookstores for out-of-print photography books and medical illustrations. Soon you will find her wandering the beaches of California as her family plans a move there in 2010. Kristen loves the smell of hardcover books, striped tights, polka dot anything, Polaroid film and pie.
Visit Kristen at www.violethour.squarespace.com.

**Ruth Rae** is an artist, author and instructor who dwells in Claremont, California, with her husband and their two teenagers, along with three dogs. Most days you will find Ruth in her studio sewing, while surrounded by vintage books, hand-dyed fabric and beads that inspire her to create. Visit Ruth at www.ruthrae.com.

**Judy Wise** is a painter, printmaker and mixed-media artist who teaches creativity workshops across the United States and abroad. In addition to product licensing and book illustration, her work has been published in a variety of books, including *Taking Flight*, *Creative Time and Space*, *Embracing Encaustic*, *1000 Journal Pages* and *Interactive Art Workshop*. She is a passionate lover of all things artful and of helping others find joy in the process of self-expression. Visit Judy at www.judywise.blogspot.com.

**Susan Tuttle** resides in a small Maine town. She has a passion for photography and creating digital art, and she enjoys making collage, abstract paintings, assemblage and altered art with found imagery and recycled objects. Susan's art has been exhibited in galleries around the United States and can be found in private collections both in the United States and abroad. She is the author of *Exhibition 36* and *Digital Expressions*. She is a frequent contributor to Stampington & Company publications and a variety of other mixed-media books. Susan teaches a series of online digital photography and digital art workshops called VisualPoetry. Visit Susan at www.ilkasattic.com or on her blog at www.ilkasattic.blogspot.com.

# INDEX

# ABOUT LIZ

Liz Lamoreux was ten when she began sewing as part of her summer involvment with the local 4-H program. Although the other girls created mid-1980s inspired miniskirts, she created a calico skirt and matching drawstring bag because she wanted to look like Laura Ingalls. During her teens, her creative focus was on writing and surrounding herself with books that became her best friends. After graduating from the University of Notre Dame, her soul-searching adventures transported her into the world of poetry, yoga and meditation.

In the last few years, she has found herself drawn to the stories told by images from her childhood—vintage handkerchiefs, bowls of seashells, glass bottles and her grandmother's sewing basket. She believes that unearthing our stories and sharing them through creating, writing and community are vital to connecting with the journey that is this life. She lives with her husband, daughter and their golden retriever, Millie, in a small house just the right size for their little family, in the beautiful Pacific Northwest, where she can often be found in her studio surrounded by strips of fabric, vintage buttons, several idea and poetry journals and a mug of tea. As a yoga teacher and artist, she sees creating as a meditative exercise for the spirit and is currently focusing on sharing this inward journey with others. Find out more about her adventures at www.lizlamoreux.com.

# DISCOVER MORE INSPIRATION WITH THESE NORTH LIGHT TITLES

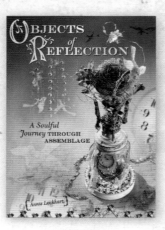

## TAKING FLIGHT
*Kelly Rae Roberts*

In *Taking Flight*, you'll find inspiration to grow your creative wings. Learn the mixed-media painting techniques Kelly Rae Roberts employs to create her artwork, including layering paints and incorporating meaningful phrases. Follow prompts to begin your own creative journey—look for the sacred in the ordinary and embrace your fears, then incorporate what you find into your art. Take further inspiration from gallery projects by the author and contributors. Spread your artistic wings and make art of your own!

ISBN-10: 1-60061-082-X
ISBN-13: 978-1-60061-082-0
paperback, 128 pages, Z1930

## OBJECTS OF REFLECTION
*Annie Lockhart*

*Objects of Reflection* embodies visual journaling disguised in the form of dimensional assemblage by creating art that is so personal it resembles a page from the artist's journal. Inspiration pours from every page of the book through a gallery of projects designed by the author. In addition, over 20 step-by-step techniques include tips for attaching elements with simple materials like string, wire and tape, aging objects, adding texture with modeling paste and more. You'll learn how to tell your own stories through your art as you turn symbolic objects into "words."

ISBN-13: 978-1-60061-331-9
ISBN-10: 1-60061-331-4
paperback, 128 pages, Z2974

## DIGITAL EXPRESSIONS
*Susan Tuttle*

Imagine flying through an inky night sky tethered to a red, heart-shaped balloon. Now imagine expressing that dream artistically. With Digital Expressions you can take ordinary photos and, with the help of Adobe Photoshop Elements, voice your flights of fancy. *Digital Expressions* guides you through 25 digital art projects created with Adobe Photoshop Elements. With this easy-to-follow guide, you'll get inspired to tackle all kinds of digital mixed-media techniques using stock photography, custom brushes, textured backgrounds and your own digital photos.

ISBN-10: 1-60061-454-X
ISBN-13: 978-1-60061-454-5
paperback, 144 pages, Z3940

## CREATIVE AWAKENINGS
*Sheri Gaynor*

*Creative Awakenings* is the key to opening the doors to your hopes and dreams, showing you how to use art making to set your intentions. Creativity coach Sheri Gaynor will be your guide through the mileposts of this exciting journey. You'll learn a variety of mixed-media techniques and a tear-out Transformation Deck will aid you in setting your intentions. You'll also get inspiration from twelve artists who share their own experiences and artwork created with the Art of Intention process.

ISBN-10: 1-60061-115-X
ISBN-13: 978-1-60061-115-5
paperback, 144 pages, Z2122

*These and other fine F+W Media titles are available from your local craft retailer, bookstore, online supplier, or, visit our Web site at www.mycraftivitystore.com.*